REJECTION

JUNKIES

by

DR. GARY L. LAWRENCE

PUBLISHED BY GLS PUBLISHING

FORWARD
BY

FLORENCE LITTAUER

BEST-SELLING AUTHOR

Every personality has strengths and weaknesses. When we experience rejection, we tend to function in, and focus on, our weaknesses.

"Rejection Junkies" enables every personality to discover the cause and cure for the rejection patterns in their lives.

In Dr. Lawrence's words, "Opposites attract, then they attack, then they retract."

In reading this book, I identified many areas in which my husband Fred and I had rejected each other in the past. We have seen first-hand how rejection exacts a tremendous toll on relationships as we have traveled around the world teaching personalities.

You too will be able to identify, isolate, and eliminate rejection patterns that prevent you from getting along with difficult people in your family, workplace, and church.

DEDICATION

For over thirty years, my wife Sylvia has loved me, encouraged me, and challenged me. This book is dedicated to her and our two sons, Gary Duane and Kevin Scott, my lovely daughter-in-law, Linda Lee, and last, but not least, my beautiful, precious granddaughters, Ashley Nicole and Kayla Danielle.

I love you all so very much!

SPECIAL THANKS

To Rose Sweet, my Choleric-Sanguine friend, who took **"Rejection Junkies"** and "colored" the pages with her special talents.

To Bill Amundson, my friend and business partner of eight years. Without his faithful, unswerving loyalty and encouragement, this edition of **"Rejection Junkies"** would have never been produced.

To Bonnie Amundson who took this "diamond in the rough" transcript and, with her X-ray vision, turned it into a masterpiece of easy, creative reading.

To all my clients and students I have been privileged to counsel. Your lives have become the canvas on which the manuscript of **"Rejection Junkies"** was painted. Thank you for allowing me to be your mentor.

TABLE OF CONTENTS

ABOUT THE AUTHOR

Dr. Gary Lawrence founded **New Life Dynamics Counseling Center** in 1980. Since its inception, NLD has counseled over 10,000 clients. As president, Dr. Lawrence has personally met with over 6,000 clients and spent an estimated 27,000 hours teaching the timeless principles represented on the pages of this book. In its seventh printing, **"Rejection Junkies"** has already sold over 20,000 copies.

Based on these thousands of hours of practical experiences, Dr. Lawrence has created many resources (books, tapes, workshop materials) in the area of mental and emotional freedom. He is also the host of the popular radio program "Common Sense Counseling," which airs daily in Phoenix, Arizona.

Gary and Sylvia Lawrence and their staff are committed to providing effective, directive, and short-term counseling that changes lives permanently.

For more information on New Life Dynamics Counseling Center or on how to schedule Dr. Lawrence as a speaker for your event, contact:

Gary Lawrence Seminars, Inc.
(602) 241-9735
(800) 373-3495
email: info@nld.org

PREFACE

This book has one solitary purpose – to communicate to you some very basic truths.

These truths which will enable you to

- *IDENTIFY*
- *ISOLATE*
- *ELIMINATE*

the **root cause** of your emotional conflicts.

Through these pages, you will get acquainted with my family and me and you will begin to understand the **Rejection Syndrome** and how it affects everyone.

You will also discover the timeless principles that I embrace. In a world where everything is constantly changing, consider this: standards change, *principles* don't change.

Much information in print today is no more than Band-Aid therapy because it addresses the *symptoms*, but ignores the *root cause* . . . the disease!

This is like the patient who is losing his eyesight and receives a prescription for stronger lenses, when the real problem is a brain tumor. How foolish! Yet, the largest percentage of counseling techniques today embraces the Band-Aid therapy philosophy.

At New Life Dynamics Counseling Center, we locate the tumor, trace its ugly tentacles and position the client for lifesaving "emotional surgery". Only then can we free the patient from the agonizing, slow, emotional "death" he has helplessly felt approaching.

My grandmother had a teakettle that whistled when the water reached the boiling point. The whistle was the signal it was time to turn off the heat. You reach your boiling point when there's a steady stream of mental and emotional turmoil in your life. This turmoil is the signal it's time to locate the source of the "heat" and turn it off! This book will help you do just that.

Understanding and acting on the truths presented in this book changed *my* life. Your life can change too!

This is my hope and expectation for you.

INTRODUCTION

A COMMON DESIRE

Many sincere Christians desire to leave past failures and frustrations behind. The Apostle Paul admonishes us to "...forget those things which are behind, and reach forth unto those things which are before." Philippians 3:13(b).

Paul is encouraging us to move forward in our maturity. That's good advice! In fact, it's great! Yet, how many times have you experienced victory in some area of your life, and the very next day suffered defeat in another area?

Perhaps that problem you had with depression, anger, fear, or feelings of inadequacy, inferiority, and insecurity has raised its ugly head again. You know that being a Christian is supposed to be a wonderful experience, but inside you are still miserable.

What is happening? What is going on?

The Bible says, "The truth shall make you free." You believe it, but you're not experiencing it. You know that for some reason you're still imprisoned emotionally, and your weaknesses are like bars that hold you back. Why aren't things changing? Where are the love, joy, and peace that Jesus promised and which you so desperately desire?

Do you want the answer?

As you read on, be forewarned - it may be *you* I'm talking about. *You* may be a **Rejection Junkie!**

A what? *A Rejection Junkie.*

1

As with alcohol, marijuana, cocaine, and other drugs, this kind of junkie unconsciously develops a dependency or an addiction to rejection. Without an awareness of what's happening, **he becomes hooked on the rejection that others give him**. Eventually, he cannot function without it. How does he become hooked?

By the time a person is eight years old, approximately 80 percent of his behavior patterns have been established. The environment in which a child is reared affects him for the rest of his life. For example, if a person is reared in a hostile environment where rejection is obvious, he usually develops in one of two ways:

1) He becomes dominant and hostile out of the need for self-preservation, or

2) He becomes extremely passive in an effort to escape any involvement in the rejection.

Very few, if any, individuals come out of this type of environment emotionally balanced.

Let's look at an example of an early emotional pattern that developed as a result of obvious rejection. In response to the hostile environment, one person will yell loudly and make demands to get what he needs, while another may choose to clam up while inwardly he continues to seethe and boil. In either case, he is developing a strong negative emotional response pattern. Like a volcano, he is now ready for an eruption. The emotional lava may explode violently or flow slowly and steadily; but one way or the other, it will come out! May God have mercy on the woman he marries! These patterns of behavior, established in early childhood, remain with a person for the rest of his life.

2

It is not unusual for a hostile, dominant type to marry a hostile, passive, inhibited type. My childhood environment was one of hostility. My wife's environment was a combination of hostility and passivity. I became a dominant, hostile person that would be in charge and my wife, Sylvia, came forth totally passive and withdrawn. She needed someone to dominate her, and I needed someone to dominate. Like two misshapen puzzle pieces, we had an emotional setup that continued to feed the rejection patterns developed in our early childhood.

This example could be reversed. The wife may emerge as the dominant, hostile partner while the husband becomes the passive, inhibited mate. Either way, both are *Rejection Junkies.*

This Book Brings Good News!
From the alcoholic or drug addict whose environment has been, and is, filled with rejection to the successful businessman who experiences rejection on a more subtle level, **Rejection Junkies can be helped!** Yes, Rejection Junkies come from every walk of life ... they are even in the churches. As a former pastor, I can tell you that they wear many disguises.

Even though a person is a Christian, the patterns of rejection are still there. The Apostle Paul tells us, "...I find then a law that, when I would do good, evil is present with me..." Romans 7:21. The 'law of the flesh' is powerful! Just like the law of gravity affects the whole human race, so does the law of the flesh. The law of the flesh is often misunderstood. Perhaps a paraphrase of the information in Romans 7:21 will help, "...I find a principle of truth, that when I want to do right, the pattern or habit of doing wrong (the law of the flesh) is still there." (Parentheses added.)

3

For example, before I became a Christian, I had a bad temper. Unfortunately, after I became a Christian, I still had a bad temper. Even though Christians have the Holy Spirit living in them, the flesh, which is the mental, emotional, and physical aspect of our being, continues to act out old habits and patterns of behavior. A person who feels inferior before becoming a Christian may still feel inferior afterward. A person who worries may still worry; the angry, hostile person may still be hostile and angry; the depressed person may continue to suffer depression even though he is a Christian.

A good illustration of this "law of the flesh" is frog legs frying in a skillet. After the frog is dead, the legs will still literally flex and jump while cooking. That is the way the 'law of the flesh' works.

The Bible says, "...Knowing this, that our old man **is crucified** with Him..." Romans 6:6(a). When a person becomes a Christian, the old nature, or self, dies. The problem is the old mental, emotional, and physical patterns continue to flex and make Christians *feel* just as much in bondage as they were before they accepted Jesus Christ as Savior. Although they now have the Holy Spirit living in them, they *feel* the same negative emotions.

The earth's law of gravity has been escaped briefly by astronauts who experienced the freedom of outer space. However, have you noticed the astronauts always return? The powerful pull of your emotional patterns cannot only be escaped, but permanently eliminated, never to pull you down again!

On to Freedom!
The flesh brings bondage but the Spirit brings freedom for eternity ... freedom from self ... freedom from others ... now! Jesus Christ has pardoned the captives and broken the chains

4

of bondage. This book will help you untangle and remove those chains and push open the doors of your emotional prison.

You can obtain and maintain your mental and emotional freedom **and live complete in Jesus Christ. The addiction** – *the bondage to rejection* - **can be history!**

1

THE AGE OF ADDICTION

"Get them while they are young and they will serve you to their death." This indoctrination philosophy is embraced by the world's most powerful political and religious systems. Whether the purpose is for good or evil, the early years of a person's life prove to be the most fertile for training the mind and emotions.

Similarly, as a result of many years of counseling experience and personal observation, I say, "Feed them *rejection* while they're young and they will become addicted to *rejection* for the rest of their lives."

There are four major areas in which we are meant to grow: the physical, intellectual, spiritual, and emotional. Maturing in each area can be sequential if that one area of development follows another; or it can be simultaneous, when each area matures at the same time and at about the same rate as the others. Let's take a look at these four growth areas and later we'll see how rejection can stunt our emotional growth, laying the foundation for future addiction.

Physical Maturity
Physical maturity is more commonly known as the aging process. Simply put, we are getting older all the time. Look in the mirror. You may notice you don't have the same body you strutted around in when you were a teenager. You may have a few more wrinkles, more gray hairs or maybe less hair. The firmness of youth is being replaced with the flabbiness of maturity. The sure quickness of youth is giving way to the purposeful, cautious steps of adulthood. To help

you understand the aging process, consider *my* view of living through the decades of life.

The Tricky Twenties
Surviving the turmoil of my teens and reaching the age of twenty was a real treat. Back then, I was almost legal age at twenty, proud that I was almost old enough to join the military and die for my country; in one more year I could vote and help decide who would sit in the White House and lead our nation. My twenties were tricky years, though. I'd listened to others' advice since I was born, and now was burdened with the task of making decisions that would affect me all my life. I was ready to strike out on my own. Let's see. Do I go to college? Get married? Have children? Take that job? Travel abroad? Join the French Foreign Legion? What *shall* I do? So many questions, but I think I know what I'm doing. I do know one thing for sure; *I don't want to end up like my parents.*

The Threatening Thirties
While the tricky twenties gave me the opportunity to lay the foundation for future decades, turning thirty was a threat. My youth was beginning to disappear and hairline cracks in my foundation were already appearing. I needed to settle down to the business of raising the children, buying groceries, and making the mortgage payment. I made sure my life insurance was paid up, trying to fight feelings of failure that, if in the event of my early demise, my precious wife and sons would be better off financially *without* me than *with* me.

The Fearful Forties
Approaching forty was fearful. All the questions I had so confidently answered in my twenties were coming back to haunt me. Had I made the right choices? Did I take the right road? Maybe I *should* have joined the French Foreign Legion. The dawn of my early years of life were turning into

the dusk of contemplation. The 'fearsome forties' was becoming a decade of reflection and readjustments. Would I ever reach my goals? If I did, what then? Making sense of all the daring and carefree decisions I had made in my youth was, to say the least, very difficult. And yet, facing these fears helped me begin reconciliation with the past.

This is usually the period in our lives in which we notice that, contrary to what we hoped, things *just don't get better with time*. We begin to ask ourselves, "Who am I? What am I doing here and where am I going?" We may respond in one of three ways.

➤ *Continue In Denial*
We stop to ask the questions, but seeing the changes we might have to make, we quickly move on, busying ourselves in our daily routine. Regrets, lost hopes and dreams are buried, and we continue our sail down the River Denial. Change is too fearful, too much work. Winston Churchill noted, "Most people some time in their lives stumble across the truth. They get up, brush themselves off and hurry quickly on their way." Life continues unchanged through our fifties, sixties and beyond, as we miss forever the deep joy those years could have offered us.

➤ *Engage In Band-Aid Therapy*
In our self-examination we may bravely change our jobs, get divorced, have affairs, or get our faces lifted. Hoping for help, some of us get into therapy. We learn to make 'I' statements and to 'fight fairly', and for awhile things seem better. But somehow the problems never really disappear because we've only treated the symptoms and not the cause. The years advance, and we lose the energy to try any more.

9

➣ *Gain Our Mental and Emotional Freedom*

Through the grace of God we learn to free ourselves mentally and emotionally and become the creature our Father intended us to be. It is this path we take that leads us to true maturity.

The Fabulous Fifties

In my own life, this decade has brought me mental and emotional freedom to enjoy life like I've never dreamed. Now that I have entered the fabulous fifties, it's with anticipation instead of regret and bitterness.

Already I know this is going to be a good and gracious time of my life. The effects of the past three decades are reconciled and life is calm. Most of the serious mistakes are in the past. I have survived the eager foolishness of youth. I am free to find pleasure in watching my adult children rear my grandchildren. It's their turn to buy the groceries and tell the kids to turn the lights out if they're not using them.

Grandchildren are not a reminder of growing older but a milestone of maturity that marks the progress I have made. Someone once said, "Fifty is the old age of youth and the youth of old age." The only thing that doesn't change is the fact that things are changing. We're all getting older. No one or nothing will reverse the process. As we mature through the fifties, it is here that we have the wisdom to repair and strengthen the foundation formed in earlier years.

The Sexy Sixties

The sexy sixties are coming soon! Many I have counseled, and who are now mentally and emotionally free, have rediscovered the warm embrace of their lover. The gentle kiss. The tender touch. The warm glow of a smile. The waking smell of freshly brewed coffee and charming chatter over the breakfast table.

One lady in her sixties shared, "Getting free mentally and emotionally from the past has brought my husband and me almost to heaven." Imagine that! A heavenly relationship while still bound in earthly, aging bodies. She went on with a thrill in her voice, "My husband tells me I'm beautiful and it sends a chill down my spine and gives me goose bumps."

Single people in their sixties have rediscovered the flame of friendships and the joy of encouraging others. They've learned loneliness is not meant to be an enemy, but a minister that guides them into a life of joyful purpose and meaning. Self-pity is put away on the shelves of the past and each day becomes an opportunity for fulfillment.

The Silly Seventies
When the 'silly seventies' arrive, most people are retired and can pretty much do what they like - and get away with it. Remember when you were a teenager and did really stupid things? Your parents would comfort you saying "Don't worry, honey, all teens go through this. You will grow out of it." Well, the great thing about the seventies is that everyone excuses your behavior because of your age. Even if you don't have Alzheimer's, you can at least lay blame for your behavior on 'part-timer's disease'!

In the seventies, a lot of things are forgotten. The good thing about forgetting bad things is that your tired, aging body has more energy to enjoy life. If you are mentally and emotionally free, the 'energy thieves' of your past will have been unplugged and discarded forever. (See Chapter 11.)

The Exalted Eighties
Next comes the 'exalted eighties'. From the lofty perch of respect for the aged, you have the advantage of being cared for by others instead of providing for them. Although many choose to focus on the aging who are tragically neglected, this is a time in our lives to be comfortable, not comatose.

You should be writing your memoirs, not your obituary. It's in this decade that our old enemy Mr. Death thins the crowd of surviving spouses and friends. If you live long enough, and want information about the 'nasty nineties', just call our toll-free number 1-800-I-LOVE-IT!

While speaking to a group of counseling clients, I shared my concern on aging. I told them my eyesight was dim, my hair was thin and gray. Besides that, I'm deaf in one ear and, depending on who's speaking and what they're saying, I can become deaf in both ears!

As my body continues to deteriorate, I'm sure my bifocals will become trifocals and, eventually I'll be wearing Coke-bottle lenses. I'll probably lose my hair and teeth and have to get dentures and a toupee. I know I won't be too proud for hearing aids because I wouldn't want to miss any tableside conversations in noisy restaurants.

When I go to bed at night, where will I put all those extra accessories I'd have accumulated? One smart student solved my dilemma. He perked up; "Get a bigger night stand!" Oh the brilliance of youth takes another bite out of the joy of aging. Would you agree that the process of aging has a humor all its own?

Intellectual Maturity
Our minds, if normal, will begin before birth to collect information. Like a computer, we store every tidbit of information in our mental data banks for future retrieval. Unfortunately, as we get older our ability to retrieve data decreases.

To fully understand the capacity of the human mind is as impossible to grasp as to understand everything Jesus did while on earth. We are told, "And there are also many other things that Jesus did, the which, if they should be written every one, I suppose that even the *world itself* could not contain the books that should be written. Amen." John 21:25. In the same way, the human mind cannot be fully explained. It still remains one of the most mysterious frontiers of discovery for modern science.

Let's talk about what we do know. We know we learn and we forget. Compared to five, ten, or even twenty years ago, it's certain you know more now than you did then. You have also forgotten a vast majority of what you did learn. Good or bad, the experiences and education of life have provided you a vast resource of knowledge from which to draw.

However, we don't necessarily get wiser as we get older. We do possess more knowledge though. Simply put, our intellectual maturing process is continuous. Formal education, or the lack thereof, has nothing to do with it; even the simplest experiences can stimulate our intellect.

We learn from reading the newspaper or the Bible, watching TV, grooming the dog, observing the stars, savoring a sunset, seeing a baby crawl, taking swimming lessons, playing golf, driving a car, making love, sharing a story, going to church, crying, and watching people. Our every waking hour, no, our every waking *second,* is another stimulation and addition to our intellectual maturing process.

Does possessing all this knowledge grant one wisdom? No! Knowledge is a mere accumulation of facts.

> ### *Wisdom is the ability to employ knowledge*
> ### *so that it benefits mankind.*

"Wisdom is the principal thing; therefore get wisdom: and with all thy getting get understanding. Exalt her (wisdom), and she shall promote thee; she shall bring thee to honor, when thou dost embrace her. She shall give to thine head an *ornament of grace*: a crown of glory shall she deliver to thee." Proverbs 4:7-9.

God emphasizes the importance of wisdom. He especially says, "With all thy getting, get wisdom."

◊ People get an education, but they never get wisdom.
◊ People get married, but never get wisdom.
◊ People get divorced, but never get wisdom.
◊ People get a job, but never get wisdom.
◊ People become parents, but never get wisdom.
◊ People get sick, but never get wisdom.
◊ People get well, but never get wisdom.
◊ People get old, but never get wisdom!

Do you know the difference between a twenty-five-year-old fool and a fifty-year-old fool? You guessed it! Twenty-five years of foolishness. Isn't it a shame there are so many intellectual fools in the world?

But even the fool learns in an intellectual manner. The tragedy lies in that he continues learning how to be foolish. Fools continue learning how to do things the wrong way for the wrong reason.

This describes a **Rejection Junkie***: a person who has learned to survive rejection in his early years.* Even though he matures physically and intellectually, he has actually become so accustomed - even addicted - to the pattern of rejection, he persists in having a life that is filled with rejection.

Spiritual Maturity
The third level of maturity is spiritual ... *or is it?* Most Christians are taught that they are to mature spiritually as they go through life. Stop and think about that. When a

14

person accepts Jesus Christ as his Lord and Savior, the Spirit of God dwells within him. "Hereby know we that we dwell in Him, and He in us, because He hath given us of His Spirit." I John 4:13.

Not above Him or beside Him, but *in* Him.
Not a portion of His Spirit. Not a little of His Spirit.
All of His Spirit, His *perfect* Spirit, His *complete* Spirit.

If that is so, how can we grow spiritually? God says, "For in him dwelleth all the fullness of the Godhead bodily. And ye are complete in Him, which is the head of all principality and power." Colossians 2:9-10. *Imagine that!* We are **complete** in Him. Spiritually complete. That which is complete cannot be added to.

Most Christians live on a constant false guilt trip of trying to 'grow spiritually'. Christians are as complete spiritually at the time of their conversion as they ever will be. No matter what the believer tries to do, say, or think, *nothing can add* to his or her spiritual completeness in Christ. Jesus said on the cross, "It is finished," John 19:30. It's done. He did it for us. He did it *in* us. He did it *in spite* of us.

Paul says, "I am crucified with Christ: nevertheless I live; yet not I, but Christ liveth in me: and the life which I now live in the flesh I live by the faith of the Son of God, who loved me, and gave himself for me. I do not frustrate the grace of God: for if righteousness comes by the law, then Christ is dead in vain." Galatians 2:20-21.

God's telling us that if we could produce spiritual life by our works, or even if we could add to the spiritual life He gave us, then Christ's death was a waste.

15

My Grandma's cooking is a good illustration of this point. As a boy I couldn't wait to go to Grandma's house for holiday meals. Boy, could she *cook*! She had a knack for preparing and serving all the dishes at the same time – and they were all piping hot. Magically, the food would appear before us: plump, brown roasted turkey that smelled delicious; fluffy mashed potatoes, rich brown gravy, buttery beans, corn and casseroles. A huge plate of her fresh, hot homemade dinner rolls was set before us. On the kitchen counter were the desserts: Grandma's famous rhubarb pie, iced cakes, and tempting raspberry tarts. When Grandma called us and assigned our places, we'd all grab a seat and there was always room for everyone. With mouths watering, we'd sit down and the room quieted. Time to say grace. I always hoped Grandma picked someone who'd pray quickly! Eating at Grandma's was a feast fit for kings.

Now, can you imagine how Grandma would react if someone said, "Grandma, I think I'll bake the turkey some more." "I think I'll brown the dinner rolls for a few more minutes." "Let's mash the potatoes some more." Oh no! *No one* ever thought of adding to her feast. When Grandma called us to her table, everything was complete. All we had to do was enjoy.

That is the way it is with God's Spirit dwelling in us. How could we ever add to the great work the Master has completed for us and in us? You are spiritually perfect if you are a Christian. This concept may frustrate you, if you've been on the false guilt trip of trying to 'grow spiritually'. Don't reject the idea yet. I'll explain the subject of spiritual completeness thoroughly in Chapter 13: *A Soul at War.*

Emotional Maturity
This final process of maturing is illustrated on the following chart entitled *Emotional Growth of Our Lives.* Let's hear Fred and Doris' story on the subject of emotional maturity:

Fred was eighty years old and his wife, Doris, was seventy-six. They'd been married fifty-three years. After hearing our radio broadcast, Fred, a retired medical practitioner, decided to schedule an appointment for counseling. I asked Fred, "Why are you seeking counseling now, after fifty-three years of marriage?" Fred answered, "I'm healthy, and I figure I'll live to be a hundred. If I'm going to spend another twenty years with Doris, I might as well be happy. Besides, what you said on the radio makes sense."

I thought to myself, "What can I possibly say to a couple who has fifty-three years of marital experience? Where should I begin? How can I help them?"

After gathering some of their background information and allowing them to vent their frustrations, I began with the chart on the emotional growth of our lives (see next page). I said, "Fred, the bottom level represents the first eight years of our life; by the time we're eight years old about 80% of our emotional response patterns are already developed. Most people don't mature *emotionally* much past this point."

Fred put his elbows on my desk, leaned forward, and with a serious, piercing look said, "Doc, what you're telling me is that I'm an eighty-year-old, eight-year-old." Before I could respond, Doris patted him on the leg and said, "Calm down, Fred. I've been telling you for over fifty years that you act like a little boy." He became angry. She became quiet. There they were, a perfect testimony to this truth: two emotional eight-year-olds trapped in the aging, wrinkled bodies of two intelligent senior citizens.

I continued, "Fred, as you can see on the second level of the chart, by the time you were 18, you'd formed 100% of your self image. You don't think any more highly of yourself now

17

than you did 62 years ago. You've developed your self worth based on *what you've done,* not on *who you are.*"

THE GROWTH AREAS OF OUR LIVES

Intellectual   *Spiritual*

Physical   *Emotional*

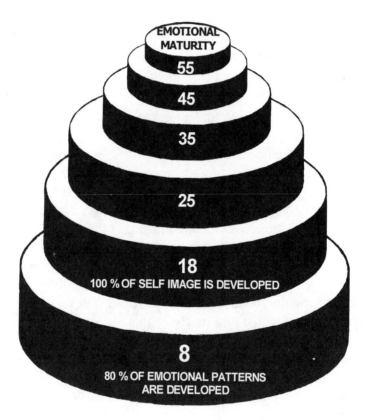

*The older we are, the less opportunity
we have to mature emotionally*

Tears began to fill Fred's eyes. I continued, "The same anger you had then you still have now. The same insecurities and anxieties you had then are still with you today. Nothing has changed except you are more educated, more financially secure, and older."

Doris reached over again and placed her right hand in his left and said, "Honey, this man does make sense." I went on, "By the time we're eighteen, most of us have been through junior high and high school. We've had teachers and others in authority telling us what our values in life should be, and then one day they presented us with a certificate of graduation. They said, 'You are the finished product of our educational system, have a great life!' So off we went. Some go to college, some to a job, and some to marriage. By the time we're twenty-five (third level on the chart), our insecurities continue to intensify. Then we become parents, continue to pay bills, buy cars, houses, and go on vacations. Rapidly we head toward age thirty-five, then forty-five, then into our fifties and sixties."

"Now, Fred, tell me, as you get physically older, what is happening to the area in which you have to mature emotionally?"

With a shocked expression, Fred replied, "It's getting smaller."

"That's right," I exclaimed, "That's precisely my point. *The older we become, the less opportunity we have to mature emotionally* because the habit of many years of child-like emotional response patterns intensifies.*"

Fred leaned back, and asked very quietly, "How do I get free of these patterns?"

Ahhh! Here we have a man, at age 80, willing to learn. Willing to change. Willing to draw on his intellectual, physical and spiritual resources so that his emotional maturing process can begin. For Fred, life begins at eighty! Most people standing at the wedding altar are emotionally-crippled eight-year-olds, *Rejection Junkies* dressed in gowns and tuxedos.

When I ask the question, "When did you notice your relationship was deteriorating?" I frequently hear the sad reply, "Before we got married." One client admitted that even during the wedding ceremony he was trying to figure out how to get an annulment.

Not one person is an exception to the fact that *eighty percent of our emotional patterns are formed by age eight.*

The simple truth is, the environment in which you are reared will affect you the rest of your life. Like rings in a tree stump, our emotional response patterns are deeply ingrained; they begin to form at birth, and are reinforced as a person responds to what life brings.

What are the four areas of maturity?

What percentage of emotional maturity is complete by age eight?

What can Christians do to grow spiritually?

MENTAL MORSEL
*"The older we are, the less opportunity
we have to mature emotionally."*

21

2

THE SIX LEVELS OF SUICIDE

Many Rejection Junkies Eventually Choose Suicide
What about the people who aren't as fortunate as Fred and never see their eighteenth birthday, much less their eightieth? Usually the emotional damage is so severe that they prematurely short-circuit, blow a fuse, and exit life via suicide. Read the newspapers: "Man Commits Suicide", "Woman Overdoses", "Teenager Hangs Himself". Maybe they were drunk or drugged. Perhaps they were bored with life, angry or depressed, or simply fearful about the future.

No matter the situation, the reason anyone commits suicide is because they were overdosed - *with rejection*. Every victim of suicide dies as a result of being a **Rejection Junkie**. Addiction to rejection begins early in life and has no preference as to when it claims its victims' lives.

There are six levels of suicide, the progressive patterns of which are often overlooked before it's too late.

Mental Suicide:
Confusion has set in and there seems to be no reasonable solution to the person's problem. Touch with reality is lost and replaced by neurosis. The inability to experience a significant purpose for life becomes all-consuming. Nothing makes sense any more.

Emotional Suicide:
This is when the ultimate, physical suicide actually begins. Thought patterns change from "This is hurting me" to "I will not feel anything".

The conflict between 'What I know' and 'What I feel' is raging: I know I'm important, but I don't *feel* important. I know I'm successful, but I don't *feel* I'm successful. I know I am loved, but I don't *feel* loved. I know I can do it, but I don't *feel* I can.

Like a header cap stops the force of spewing oil from a well, callousness covers the emotions. No pain is allowed. No release is given. The pressure builds. Even the most sincere efforts to help this person are often to no avail.

Social Suicide:
The victim begins to withdraw from normal relationships and activities with family members and friends. Contact with other people diminishes to the point of isolation. The feeling of worthlessness is at maximum level. The *truth* of what they know is plowed under by the *lies* of what they *feel*. Suicide is sensible at this point: do the world a favor and get out of its way. The victim becomes an island unto himself.

Moral Suicide:
Mentally confused, emotionally callused, and socially isolated, the victim now finds himself or herself betraying their moral values. This frequently involves some kind of substance abuse that often leads to immoral behavior with others, often with strangers. People involved in extra-marital affairs, promiscuity, or same-sex relationships will often identify with this level of suicide.

Spiritual Suicide:
A spiritual emptiness is experienced. The victim *feels* God has rejected him. He finds no solace in Christianity, for it seems not even God has the answer.

Physical Suicide:
Now that the first five stages are in operation, the stage is set for the 'Grand Finale'. *Mentally confused, emotionally*

24

callused, socially isolated, morally decimated, and spiritually bankrupt, the time has now come for the gun, the poison, the overdose, the jump, or the carbon monoxide.

The *final fix of rejection* will send a bitter message beyond the grave to surviving family and friends, "See, I showed you. Who's sorry now? I knew I'd get your attention. You could have - should have - loved me more. I hope you feel guilty."

The truth is that we couldn't convince a suicidal **Rejection Junkie** of any hope. Their mind is made up - or was made up. Suicide is not an accident. It is an incident of intention.

Very young members of society who are alone, fearful, depressed, and rejected commit suicide. In a CBS news special, it was reported over 30,000 children in the Los Angeles area were being victimized (rejected) in the child pornography business. America the Beautiful has some ugly problems. The good ol' American way of life has an alarming increase in child abuse of all sorts (rejection) in epidemic proportions. Battered babies are being buried; teenagers are tossed out of their homes; blended families from divorce and remarriage often cause competition (rejection) between stepparent and child. These children are all becoming confirmed **Rejection Junkies** and will carry the unseen mental and emotional damage into their adult lives.

Here's the real tragedy. As these victims become addicted to rejection, they'll pass it on to their children. It's tragic but true that most child abusers were also abused when they were children. From generation to generation the rejection recycles itself. (See Chapter 6.)

Can Christians Be Rejection Junkies?

Be very careful. Don't assume that you're not a Rejection Junkie just because you haven't been abused (rejected) on an overt (or obvious) open level. Many Rejection Junkies I counsel were born into, and reared in, *good* Christian homes. Many symptoms of a Rejection Junkie are obvious (overt) and very easy to spot. However, other symptoms are subtle (covert) and often much harder to identify. (See Chapter 7.)

To determine if you are a Rejection Junkie, you must personally seek the Lord. "I, the Lord, search the heart, I try the reins..." Jeremiah 17:10. He will help you objectively and honestly view your character traits and pinpoint any symptoms of the Rejection Syndrome. The most obvious of these are hostility, anxiety, depression, insecurity, and feelings of inadequacy and inferiority. The least obvious is inhibition, indifference, quietness and extreme sub-missiveness. To identify symptoms of being addicted to rejection, be willing to examine yourself. Be careful not to confuse **personality** (what you have developed on the outside) with **character** (who you truly are inside).

Let me give you those definitions again:
Personality: What you want people to think you are as a result of your behavior.
Character: What you truly are as God knows you to be. "Man looketh on the outward appearance but the Lord looketh on the heart." 1 Samuel 16:7.

What I Am About To Say May Offend Some Christians

These two statements wear me out: "I'm trusting the Lord" and "I'll keep praying about it." Please understand, I believe wholeheartedly in trusting and praying to God and am grateful for salvation through the shed blood of Jesus Christ.

But, dear friends, look around and you will see trusting, prayerful Christians by the dozens who are miserable

26

Rejection Junkies; their lives are void of the Fruit of the Spirit!

Whether a person is a Christian or not has nothing to do with the sad facts:

Christians Commit Suicide!

Christians Get Divorced!

Christians Commit Adultery!

Christians Commit Crimes!

Christians Lie!

Christians Get Depressed!

Christians Get Hostile!

Christians Withdraw!

Christians Worry!

Christians have the same problems as non-Christians!
The largest percent of my counseling clients are Christians whose lives are filled with anger, insecurity, worry, and depression. Christians are human!

Everyone experiences rejection. When a person has absorbed enough rejection throughout his life, he develops the *habit*; he gets *hooked* and eventually cannot function without it.

**Rejection addiction is no different
from any other addiction.**

For every one case that is reported (such as those who seek counseling and with whom I work primarily), there are thousands who go untreated.

Being a Rejection Junkie destroys any ability to function in an open, accepting, and loving relationship with others.

Rejection Junkies suffer through their addiction in a sad and miserable attempt to *get it all together*.

Define **personality** and **character**.

What are the six levels of suicide?

What is the difference between a Christian and non-Christian Rejection Junkie?

MENTAL MORSEL
"My weaknesses are related to my behavior and my strengths are related to my character."

29

THE ROOTS OF
BITTERNESS

3

THE BEGINNINGS OF BONDAGE

A Wounded Spirit

Nancy was only sixteen. Her psychological test indicated she was suicidal. When I asked her why she hadn't already killed herself, she replied, "There would be no one to take care of Candy!"

"Who's Candy?" I asked. She replied, "My pony." The only reason this young girl had for living was concern for her pony.

Nancy was in emotional bondage. Her test results showed her to be nervous, depressive, withdrawn, subjective, hostile, and impulsive. The first levels of suicide were already in progress. Just when did her bondage begin?

I asked Nancy, "Which of your parents do you hate the most?" Without hesitation she replied, "My dad."

I asked her why. As her story began to unfold, I learned that her father had promised to build her a swing set. This was intended as a peace offering for moving her away from her friends in the city to the isolation of country life.

While listening, I tried to reconcile the promise of a swing set and her age of sixteen. They just didn't go together. I asked her how old she was when this promise had been made. "I was nine at the time," she replied.

At age nine, Nancy had a wounded spirit because of her father's broken promise. Throughout her elementary and junior high school years, her father had disappointed her

31

repeatedly by breaking many promises. She began to feel she could never trust him again. In her mind, her father was a liar. Now she was old enough to rebel against him and do whatever she wanted whether he liked it or not.

Bitterness toward her father had put her in bondage to him. Her hatred and anger toward him controlled her mentally and emotionally every day of her life.

The Root of Bitterness

Like a lethal tumor, bitterness infects a person's life and spreads into relationships with other people, claiming a deadly hold. It worms its noxious influence into every aspect of the victim's life. Brothers and sisters become enemies. Friendships are shattered. Marriages are poisoned. Careers crumble. Churches are torn apart. Relationships between parents and children are irreparably damaged.

Bitterness is deceptive. Often it is confused with outward actions of anger and rage. However, *anger is a response; bitterness is resentment.* Bitterness is an ugly word and often clients will respond, "But I don't *feel* I'm bitter." It's important to understand that bitterness is not what you *feel*, it is the *cause* of what you feel.

The following definitions of bitterness are mine - not Webster's. However, after you've given these definitions honest, unbiased consideration, I think you'll have a more accurate understanding of what bitterness is and how it infects your life.

Bitterness is ...
- **an inward resentment**
- **a wounded spirit**
- **a fear**
- **a guilt**
- **an anxiety**
- **an avoidance**
- **a sense of loss**
- **a sense of abandonment**
- **a sense of betrayal**

If there is someone in your past or present life you inwardly resent, you are bitter. You are bitter if someone, past or present, wounded your spirit. If you have an anxiety, fear, or guilt regarding a certain person or circumstance, you are bitter. If you have a sense of loss from abandonment or betrayal, you are bitter.

Bitterness camouflages itself in many ways. Many counseling services focus on a person's actions and prescribe behavior modification to help the person cope with the dilemma. This Band-Aid therapy is like the doctor who prescribes exercise and diet for the overweight person with a thyroid tumor. The symptom of weight gain will not totally disappear until the root of the problem is eliminated and the tumor is removed.

In our counseling office we focus on the person's attitude, not his actions. We understand there are times when a person's behavior (what he *does*) will betray his character (who he *is*). How people behave in certain circumstances is not always a reliable testimony of their true character. God says, "Let all bitterness, and wrath, and anger, and clamor, and evil speaking, be put away from you, with all malice." Ephesians 4:31. Please notice that *bitterness* is listed first. When the root of bitterness is dealt with, the rest of the negative emotional response patterns cease.

Attitude gives birth to action. Before you can eliminate the confusing behavior in your life, you must be positioned to eliminate your bitterness. Right now you may be frustrated, confused, hurting, angry, depressed, withdrawn, or extremely dominant. These feelings are what you experience as a result of your bitterness.

The *root of bitterness* is the underlying cause of most mental and emotional conflict. God says, "Looking diligently lest any man fail of (miss out on) the grace of God; lest any root of bitterness springing up *trouble* you and thereby many be *defiled."* Hebrews 12:15. (Parenthesis added.)

The root of bitterness does two things - it **troubles** the individual and it **defiles** many. *You are troubled.* That's what bitterness does to the individual. *Many are defiled.* You are defiled and your defilement spreads to others.

Let's examine the word **defiled** as found in Hebrews 12:15. The original Greek word for defiled is *miaino* which means
- **to sully, taint, stain or blemish.**
- **contaminate, tinge with something injurious**
- **pollute, make impure by mixture**
- **make dishonest, open to bribery, influenced for evil**
- **pervert, make impure**

We can understand why many people choose not to lay claim to their bitterness. It's an ugly word with ugly consequences.

You may be a very nice, moral, honest and sincere person. However, the chances are that you are a very nice, moral, honest, sincere, and *bitter* person!

A *nice,* **bitter** person? Now there's an oxymoron for you. The world is full of nice (on the outside) but bitter (on the inside) people. Remember the song *"Lemon Tree"*? The words are "Lemon tree, very pretty and the lemon flower is sweet, but the fruit of the poor lemon is impossible to eat."

I don't believe in the diagnosis of mental illness unless there is a definite physiological cause such as mental retardation, chemical imbalance, brain tumor, or brain damage. I do believe in mental and emotional turmoil created by the ever-growing roots of bitterness.

Simply put, *bitterness is the beginning of bondage.*

Rejection Junkies

Remember Nancy, the suicidal teenager? She's now in her early twenties. She's already been married and divorced and still in emotional bondage to her father. Typical of the victims of the root of bitterness, she unknowingly carried her hostility, depression, and anxiety into her marriage. Shortly after the honeymoon, all the emotional response patterns she'd developed early in life began to surface in her relationship with her husband. She felt she could not really trust him and that she was not truly important to him. It seemed he could never measure up to her expectations of what a husband should be. Within two years of this rejection recycled, Nancy's husband had an affair with another woman. Nancy could now confirm her feelings that all men are alike and none of them can be trusted.

What happened? Why did the marriage end so tragically? Nancy was a Rejection Junkie! Her early years were filled with rejection from her father. Although she was never abused physically or verbally, her father did lie to her by breaking his promises. At a very young age, Nancy developed a root of bitterness by concluding that women can't trust men. When she married, she unconsciously recreated with her husband the same rejection patterns that had always existed between her and her father.

Because of Nancy's addiction to rejection, she'd developed the habit of having to have her regular *fixes*. Nancy didn't know it, but she was *shooting up* with rejection in her emotional blood stream. We might refer to her divorce as an *overdose*.

Nancy didn't consciously want that much rejection, but she had been in the habit of receiving it regardless. Where is Nancy today? Still bitter towards her father and ex-husband, still depressed and angry, still suicidal.

There are many variations to this pattern that can be identified in relationships as a result of the root of bitterness. Rejection, like a Ping-Pong ball in motion, bounces all over the place. Wives reject their husbands. Husbands reject their wives. Parents reject their children. Children reject their parents. Employers reject their employees. Employees reject their employers. Pastors reject their congregation. Church members reject their pastors.

The Age of Addiction
Rejection seems like the only game in town where everyone is qualified to play. No one escapes rejection. It bounces back and forth and into the lives of innocents with the age of addiction always starting in the early years of a person's life. I've counseled with some eight and nine-year-olds that could not function in a family relationship.

Little Billy's Rejection Syndrome began before he was born. When his mother was a child, her father overtly rejected her by slapping her and yelling at her. The only attention she received from her father was when he was angry with her. As a result of this unkind treatment, she vowed this would never happen to her children. However, the way she tried to prevent this was to overprotect, baby, and smother Billy (covert rejection) while opposing her husband's efforts at discipline.

In spite of her good intentions, the Ping-Pong game of rejection was now in effect; the syndrome was continuing from one generation to the next. Contrary to her vow, she passed the rejection that she had absorbed down to her son. When Billy was seven, his father gave up trying to discipline him because his bitter, fearful wife thwarted his every attempt. So, not only did the mother reject Billy, the father also rejected him by giving up on disciplining him. Naturally, the boy was unkind, arrogant and unruly.

REJECTION BOUNCES INTO THE LIVES OF THE INNOCENT.

A psychiatrist labeled him hyperactive, a psychologist labeled him schizophrenic, and I diagnosed him as a Rejection Junkie. Unwittingly, the mother had ensured that her son had the same relationship with his father as she had with hers - none. So Billy, a Rejection Junkie at nine years of age, was emotionally handicapped and rendered incapable of responding to authority.

When I began counseling the mother and she realized her behavior would have to change, she became threatened. They never came back. Today the couple is divorced. Their second son lives with the father and has no mother, while Billy lives without a father. Such a tragedy. Addicted in the early years of life, Billy continues in the Rejection Syndrome.

What is the beginning of mental and emotional bondage? It is the **root of bitterness**.

What is the underlying cause of most mental and emotional conflict?

Explain the difference between anger and bitterness.

What are some definitions of bitterness?

What are the two things that bitterness does?

MENTAL MORSEL

"Sometimes my behavior will betray my character."

4

SOUR GRAPES ON A DEAD VINE

The Generational Pass Down

Many things are passed down from one generation to the next. Family traditions, family businesses, religious beliefs and even ministries are passed from generation to generation. Unfortunately, the bad passes with the good just like diseases that are genetically cycled from parents to children.

Bitterness is no exception. Bitterness is visited upon the children unto the third and fourth generation. Bitterness is like sour grapes on a dead vine.

The principle of the Generational Passdown is first introduced in Exodus 20:5-6. The Israelites were given the law that God spoke to Moses and Moses spoke to the people. Regarding graven images, God said "Thou shalt not bow down thyself to them, nor serve them: for I the Lord thy God am a jealous God, visiting the iniquity of the fathers upon the children unto the third and fourth generation of them that hate me; and showing mercy unto thousands of them that love me, and keep my commandments."

Again God says, "And the Lord passed by before him, and proclaimed: the Lord, the Lord God, merciful and gracious, long-suffering, and abundant in goodness and truth; keeping mercy for thousands, forgiving iniquity and transgression and sin, and that will by no means clear the guilty; visiting the iniquity of the fathers upon the children and upon the children's children, unto the third and fourth generation." Exodus 34:6-7.

Is God saying He'll punish the innocent for the sins of the guilty? No, absolutely not!

God says He sees the rebellion and idolatry of one generation surfacing in the next and passing even into the third generation. God is not focused on the iniquity of the generations to come, but rather on *offering His mercy, love, and forgiveness to any and all generations that seek repentance.*

Sad to say, only a few (thousands) will seek God's forgiveness while the majority (multitudes) will continue in their rebellion and idolatry.

God understands the sin nature of man. He understands the inclination of children to follow their parents' lead. God is telling us, "I will show the same mercy, love and grace for each succeeding generation." He will forgive their iniquity, transgressions, and sin, but those who are guilty and choose *not* to repent, will not be cleared.

God never holds innocent people responsible for the sins of the guilty. Innocent people, however, will often suffer because of the behavior of the guilty.

So it is with bitterness. We've seen how bitterness can be passed down from our parents and their parents and their parents before them. Even if the previous generations are dead, the effect of their bitterness can be carried over into *our* lives.

While lamenting Israel's condition, the prophet Jeremiah said, "Our fathers have sinned and are not; we have born their iniquities." Lamentations 5:7. Bitterness gives birth to all forms of rebellion, idolatry, anger, depression, fear, anxiety and most all other mental and emotional maladies.

Bitterness is the vine upon which sour grapes grow. You've heard the expression about a person who's angry, resentful, or bitter described as being full of 'sour grapes'. Interestingly, this proverb originated in Israel. The Israelites charged God with injustice toward the innocent generations that suffered because of their forefathers' rebellion. They were experiencing a bad case of *sour grapes*.

God responded, "What mean ye, that ye use this proverb concerning the land of Israel, saying: The fathers have eaten sour grapes and the children's teeth are set on edge? As I live, saith the Lord God, thy children's teeth are set on edge. As I live, saith the Lord God, ye shalt not have occasion any more to use this proverb in Israel." Ezekiel 18:2-3.

God told the people to quit blaming Him, their forefathers, or others for their own condition. The message is the same to us today:

Assume responsibility for your own attitudes and actions.

God continued, "... The son shall not bear the iniquity of the father, neither shall the father bear the iniquity of the son: the righteousness of the righteous shall be upon him, and the wickedness of the wicked shall be upon him." Ezekiel 18:20. Children, quit blaming your parents; parents, quit blaming your children.

People do what they want to,
nothing more and nothing less.

The choice is yours!

The Dead Vine
God compared the Hebrew nation to a vine. "Thy mother is like a vine in thy blood, planted by the waters; she was

41

fruitful and full of branches by reason of many waters."
Ezekiel 19:10.

Israel was blessed. Her nation was as a vine reaching into the lives of every descendant. But the people's rebellion and sin borne by their bitterness caused a great tragedy. From the life-giving waters their nation was torn and cast into a dry and desolate desert.

"But she was plucked up in fury, she was cast down to the ground, and the east wind dried up her fruit; her strong rods were broken and withered; the fire consumed them. And now she is planted in the wilderness, in a dry and thirsty ground."
Ezekiel 19:12-13.

From blessing to blight. From freedom to fury. From prominence to poverty.

What will grow on the vine of life which has been cast into the desert? There are no sweet, plump, fruits of love like peace and joy, only sour grapes on a dead vine. The "sour grapes" of bitterness will be passed from generation to generation.

Are *you* eating sour grapes? Are your teeth set on edge because of your own bitterness? When you think of certain people, circumstances and experiences of the past, does your face grimace or do you grit your teeth?

The good news to each generation visited by bitterness is that they have full access to the healing love, mercy and forgiveness of God!

Some of the multitudes will avail themselves of God's love and mercy and free themselves of the bondage of bitterness. The rest will continue growing sour grapes. What will you do?

Who does God hold responsible for our attitude?

How many generations does God visit with His grace and mercy?

What is passed down from generation to generation?

MENTAL MORSEL
"When I focus on my attitude,
I cease to focus on others' actions."

5

Personality Passdown

After I'd finished my presentation at a seminar, a woman named Margaret approached me and said, "I need to talk to you!"

She angrily explained she was the mother of a nine-year-old boy and seven-year-old girl, and had been divorced for four years. Her marriage had lasted only five years, and she briefly shared some of her other parenting and personal problems. It was clear a deeply wounded spirit accompanied her anger. She snarled, "I'm also sick and tired of being treated like a piece of meat!" Margaret felt that her obvious physical beauty had worked against her because most of the men she had dated assumed that it was their right to have physical relations with her in payment for a night of dining and dancing. She was a hostile, depressed and very rejected woman.

Concerned, I asked, "Margaret, would you describe the relationship you had with your father as you were growing up?"

Still agitated, Margaret turned her focus on her dad. "He was a bitter old man. He was always angry. Mom and I could never please him. Although he was critical and demanding, Mom never fought back, but I sure did! Dad was cruel. He used to call me names like 'slut' and 'whore', and he'd pinch me on my arms when he lost his temper." I listened as the pain, built up over many years, spewed out of Margaret's wounded soul.

I asked, "Do you remember ever saying to yourself as a little girl 'I'll never be like my father'?" "Yes!" she exclaimed, "My *whole life* has been based on never being like Dad."

I responded cautiously, "Margaret, what would you say if I told you no matter who you re-marry the rest of your life, you will *never* be a happily married woman?"

"What do you mean?" she asked, surprised.

"Do you realize that in your desire to never be like your father, you have become just like him?"

"I am **not!** I'm nothing like my father, I have nothing in common with that S.O.B.!" Quietly I encouraged Margaret to hear me out.

"You've developed an 'emotional focus', Margaret. Who was it that for the past few minutes has had an angry spirit, and been critical of her father and men in general, and demanding that men perform at a certain level? Who also in disciplining her son loses her temper and becomes cruel and bitter?"

"Here's the bottom line, Margaret. You've spent so much time and energy trying not to be like your father that you have become very much like him. Although you were genuinely hurt by him, your bitterness has developed into the emotional focus toward him and your own personality has been affected."

As I continued counseling her, I explained the three-step process that occurs in the personality pass down. The first step was completed when, as a child, she developed a *despite* toward her father when her spirit was wounded. The second step was completed when Margaret *deliberated* on his weaknesses, especially through her teen years. The third and final step was inevitable: *duplication*. She had conformed to her father's emotional patterns and despite all her protests had, in fact, become very much like that S.O.B.!

When the truth of the personality pass down hit Margaret, she crumpled in heavy sobs. With her face in her hands and between tears, she choked brokenly; "I've been seeing a psychiatrist for *two years. W*hy couldn't *he* have taught me this?"

The Personality Passdown was further evidenced as Margaret began to discuss her own children. Her son was bitter because his own dad never spent time with him and angry with mom for divorcing dad. Outwardly, Margaret's son was very much like her, angry, critical and demanding. Margaret's daughter, also wounded, had turned her bitterness inward and was inhibited, indifferent and passive. The boy was obviously in the process of becoming a 'survivor' and the girl was developing as an 'escaper'.

Everyone comes out of childhood either as a 'survivor' or an 'escaper'. Personality patterns can be formed as a result of the bitterness toward our parents or others in those early years. The root of this bitterness (the inward attitude) gives birth to the personality patterns (outward actions).

Who of us doesn't have more than one emotional focus? Often they include parents, grandparents, other relatives, siblings, teachers and others in authority as we grew up. I came out of my environment as a 'survivor'. Fueled by my bitterness toward authority, I charted a course of independence and alienation from my family.

My wife, Sylvia, turned her childhood bitterness inward and, like Margaret's daughter, started down the road of passivity and dependence, typical of an 'escaper'. As you know, our marriage was based on my being in control and her being in obedience. This parent-child relationship is evidenced to some degree in every marriage.

Margaret's story is quite common among Christians. Divorce rates are rampant and shocked, hurt, confused, and broken families are all asking, "What happened?"

The Personality Passdown can't be eliminated until the **bondage of bitterness** is broken.

What is the three-step process that occurs in the Personality Passdown?

List five people you have developed an emotional focus toward.

MENTAL MORSEL
*"A child is a mirrored reflection
of the parents' attitudes and actions."*

49

6

REJECTION RECYCLED

I frequently ask clients, "When did you first notice problems in your marriage?" Although the answers vary, I often hear "On our wedding day!"

Why is it that so often, before the couple can carry their baggage into the honeymoon suite, the relationship is *already falling apart*?

The reason is simple; new nighties and champagne aren't the only items in their luggage! Those suitcases are packed with massive rejection heaped upon the bride and groom often from the time they were born. *Excess baggage* of rejection and its emotional response patterns gets carried from childhood directly into marriages, where the *rejection is recycled*.

Rejection usually causes one of two general reactions; one is *passive* and the other is *aggressive*.

Inversion occurs when a person demonstrates behavior patterns of withdrawal. Some symptoms are extreme quietness, lack of showing affection or expression, depression, inhibitions, indifference, isolation, distancing and passivity.

Reversion occurs when a person demonstrates behavior patterns of anxiety, hostility, verbal or physical attacks, relentless pursuing and aggressiveness.

The inverter withdraws from the relationship for safety, or "distances". The reverter, however, pursues the distancer to cast his anger upon him. The old cat-and-mouse game is in full swing! The more the reverter (cat) pursues, the more the inverter (mouse) increases the distance. The quieter the inverter becomes, the louder the reverter rages!

THE CAT IS THE REVERTER, THE MOUSE IS THE INVERTER

What is going on here? At first glance, it may appear that the more powerful one in the relationship is the loud, aggressive reverter. The quiet inverter appears to be the innocent victim. By refusing to respond openly and directly, the quiet, withdrawn, passive/aggressive inverter often wields the greater control. The inverter tries to control in order that there will be no chaos or conflict. Since it takes two to fight, they control by just going away.

The reverter's emotional response to rejection is to gain control in an open manner, either by verbal or physical force. When the passive inverter goes limp emotionally, there's no fight left for the aggressive reverter to win. So he loses. Each of us responds to rejection in an effort to control our environment, but in opposite ways.

It's sad; two people fighting in different ways for control; two people, *both losing*, both recycling rejection. Let's take a look at some of the most common patterns of recycled rejection in marriage:

Dominant Husband vs. Passive Wife

This phrase describes my wife, Sylvia, and me. Our rejection of each other began to be recycled even before we were married. I'd been the baby of my family and overprotected by my mother, which as you recall is a form of covert rejection.

I was a sickly child, had undergone numerous surgeries and saw myself as a skinny, flop-eared runt. I could never compete with my popular older brothers who were the jocks in school and who both ended up joining the Marines. In my pre-adolescent years, my father continually physically and verbally attacked me. In my teens, though, I began to fight back. I was a bitter, angry young man.

As a maturing *Rejection Junkie,* I started recycling the rejection I'd received. I pushed my over-protective mother away in hope of gaining my father's acceptance. That didn't work, because, unknown to me, he had never believed he was my real father! Of course he was, but that didn't change the fact I had no healthy relationship with either parent. I'd survive all this but later in my marriage I'd revert this rejection onto my wife.

I was 22 when I met Sylvia. We were different in personality but had similar backgrounds of rejection. Her mother was hostile and abusive. Her father, who never raised his voice, was quiet and reserved. Sylvia grew up in fear of her mother's anger. When mother issued orders, they were to be obeyed immediately and perfectly. Any infractions of these rigid rules were met with mother's vengeance.

Seldom did Sylvia's father intervene or express his feelings. Neither parent expressed love to Sylvia, who began to withdraw. Sylvia decided not to fight back because it wouldn't be worth the pain. Sylvia would do whatever it took to survive, to *escape* mentally and emotionally, and later in our marriage she would repeat her performance.

Can you see how the rejection patterns were set long before we met? I needed to dominate someone and Sylvia needed someone to dominate her. We were a perfect match - two *Rejection Junkies* shooting each other up with daily fixes of rejection! I rejected Sylvia by making all of her decisions for her; she rejected herself, and me, by letting me! After a four-month courtship, I told Sylvia she needed to marry me, so she did. The first two years of our marriage were filled with my shouting, cursing, slamming doors, breaking things and demanding everything be done my way, or else.

I was the cat; Sylvia was the mouse. One day, though, the little mouse had had enough! Sylvia decided she would fight back, and she literally tore into me, kicking, screaming, scratching and hitting. The angrier she was, the quieter I became. Now she was the cat and I became the mouse.

What was happening? *I had finally succeeded in getting her to reject me the way I was used to being rejected!* Since we both overdosed on rejection, I had forced her into becoming the reverter, while I slipped into my old childhood role of being massively rejected by my parents (Sylvia). I now had the overt rejection I'd had as a child.

Sylvia also unconsciously tried to get me to reject her on the covert level of her childhood. Often when I'd compliment her or tell her I loved her, Sylvia would reply that I didn't really mean it, that I was only saying that because husbands were supposed to say those things to their wives. After trying to convince her for a year and a half that she *was* the most

54

beautiful woman I'd ever met and that I *did* love her, she *still* didn't believe me. Well, fine! I told her I wouldn't *ever* compliment her again!

There it goes! The Ping-Pong ball of rejection was bouncing back and forth totally out of control. We continued for a long time like this - recycling rejection.

Dominant Wife vs. Passive Husband

Jim was the passive husband while Diane had become the dominant wife. Married for thirty years, their relationship had deteriorated to the point that they simply tolerated each other. In Diane's childhood, her father had abandoned the family. Diane's mother was then forced to work long hard hours in a factory, while Diane and her younger sister went to live with an aunt and uncle. The two girls had to work after school and on weekends in their uncle's restaurant. During her school years there was only time for work and study.

Discipline was strict. The only praise Diane received was for a good job cleaning the house, doing laundry or working at the restaurant. *Diane began to gain her self esteem from what she did, not from who she was.* Diane also began to be determined that she would be successful, no matter what, and that she'd never end up like her mother, married to a man who wouldn't provide for her.

Jim and Diane met during their senior year in high school. He was kind, gentle, and worked hard at school and his part-time job. With their busy schedules, Jim and Diane only had one evening together on weekends.

Jim had been the only child of a passive father and dominant mother. As is common with an only child or even the baby of the family, he experienced covert rejection by over-protection. His mother made all the decisions for Jim. His

55

father worked for the railroad and was usually gone. When father was home, he was tired and remained uninvolved in family activities. Jim's father allowed his wife to take care of the home, the children and the finances. Because her husband was usually away, Jim became an emotional 'surrogate spouse' to his mother, listening as she discussed her problems with him.

Jim's mother complained of being rejected by her husband. She tried to teach Jim that a good husband is thoughtful of his wife's needs and if he really loves her, he'll provide for her and always have a good, steady job.

With father usually away from home and withdrawn when he *was* home, and with Mother being rather 'long suffering', Jim rarely heard his parents argue. Being comfortable with mother making all his decisions and taking care of things, Jim also felt comfortable with Diane. Like his mother, Diane was a hard worker, very decisive and certain about what she wanted out of life. They married right out of high school.

Six years and two children later, their marriage had become identical to that of Jim's parents. Jim worked six days a week while Diane ran the house, handled the finances, and raised the children. Diane saw her responsibility as raising children who grew up to be successful. Jim saw his responsibility as providing financially for the family. Diane prided herself on her own ability to handle so much but became increasingly resentful that Jim didn't do more to meet her and the children's needs other than bringing home the paycheck.

After eighteen years, the marriage had become totally non-sexual and void of any romance, but Diane decided to stick it out 'for the kids' sake'. Jim rarely made any decisions. Like clockwork, he just kept getting up each day and going to work, providing for his family.

56

After the children left home, Diane became active at church, where she felt needed and appreciated. Jim kept on working and providing for the home. After thirty years, Diane hit her limit. She wanted out. That was fine with Jim because he still had his job. They divorced.

Unconsciously Diane created the same rejection in her life that her mother experienced - no husband. Diane went to work in a restaurant because she wasn't trained for anything else. Divorced, Jim and Diane now live alone, and their children take turns visiting one or the other on holidays. Two more Rejection Junkies recycling the rejection.

Passive Husband vs. Passive Wife
Bill and Cathy were married twenty-eight years. Their three children were grown, out on their own, and Bill and Cathy were left with a painfully empty, dull, and lifeless marriage. The results of their psychological tests showed they were both extremely nervous, depressive, inhibited, indifferent and overly submissive. Finally, Cathy told Bill that something had to be done because she couldn't stand it anymore. Bill agreed and, true to his passive nature, suggested *she* see what *she* could do about the problem.

During counseling, I learned Cathy had been a 'late in life' baby. Her father was 55 and her mother was 44 and the sole purpose of Cathy's birth was to pump new life into their dull marriage. When she was six months old, however, they divorced. All of her life, Cathy felt guilty for failing her assigned mission which was to save her parents' marriage.

Most of her pre-school days were spent idly playing in her room while mother whirled through social circles. This fast-paced life was possible for Cathy's mother because grandma was a built-in babysitter. Cathy was a good child and seldom misbehaved. In high school she was not allowed to date

57

because mother didn't want her to 'get hurt' like she'd been hurt. Cathy felt unpopular in school because she wasn't pretty. Without the courage, or encouragement, to get involved in school activities, Cathy had no friends. Her quiet life revolved around only two people, mother and grandmother.

Bill was one of the boys in Cathy's neighborhood. They never dated, but Bill and Cathy grew up seeing each other often at school. Bill was also a good boy, but being overweight and feeling self-conscious, rarely socialized. Bill's focus turned to academics and his goal of becoming an electronic engineer. His parents gave him no affection, but praised him for his good grades. Bill and Cathy both had become loners.

Bill entered junior college in their hometown, and Cathy left for nursing school in a nearby city. The first summer they were home for vacation, they began to notice each other. They began dating and their relationship was quiet and comfortable. They agreed they'd wait for Cathy to graduate before marrying so she could work and help Bill finish school. After the wedding, that's exactly what happened. Cathy went to work and Bill went to school.

After the kids came, there wasn't much time left to build a marriage. The covert rejection patterns of their childhood were so strong that neither Bill nor Cathy showed much affection to each other or their children. They did, however, provide a quiet home where the environment was one of work, study and sleep, with a vacation every five years.

Unlike overt rejection, covert rejection can be more tolerable for a longer period of time.

It took twenty-eight years for one of the Rejection Junkies to want to break the cycle badly enough to *do* something about it!

The good news is that Bill and Cathy are now living a life of joy, freedom and fulfillment. As a result of understanding and responding to the principles learned in counseling Bill and Cathy's communication has skyrocketed, and their marriage is filled with a new intimacy. *Rejection Junkies can break the habit if they want to!*

Dominant Husband vs. Dominant Wife
Because of the constant struggle for power within the relationship, and the intensity that usually accompanies it, this combination is a "rare breed". With no mouse to chase, these two alley cats will fight to the end. The death of the marriage is usually swift and savage. Although we usually don't find this couple in the counselor's office, they are like the others who continually recycle rejection.

What is inversion?

What is reversion?

List the four examples of rejection recycled in relationships.

MENTAL MORSEL

"Repetition can be the greatest teacher
or the greatest torture."

7

IT IS REJECTION WHEN ...

I'm sure that some of you reading this book are thinking, "I've never been rejected." Not so! *Everyone experiences rejection on some level.* The problem comes when a person has absorbed so much rejection he unconsciously recreates it in his relationships with others.

You have been rejected, although you may not realize it! Remember, there are two types of rejection - overt and covert.

Overt rejection is very obvious, like yelling, screaming, hitting, dirty looks, and carries the message that a person is unwanted or unloved. This form of rejection is usually intentional and acted out in intensely emotional situations.

Covert rejection is not so obvious, often very subtle, and experienced most often in an "unseen" manner. Always being busy, lack of physical touch, spoiling a child, and not teaching the kids about sex are all forms of covert rejection. This type of rejection is usually not intentional, and many times is the result of circumstances in one's environment over which there is no control. Emotional upheavals are not normally a part of covert rejection because the victim isn't as likely to read it as rejection at the time.

Of the two types, covert rejection is the most difficult to deal with. Why? Because the victims are usually in a state of denial, and actually comfortable with the familiarity of their learned behavior patterns. To change would require the victim to leave an established "emotional safety zone" and take action on the problem, which is not always easy.

The following categorized illustrations will reveal the many ways in which we experience **covert** rejection. Some of them may seem humorous or strange but, *to the victim,* they are quite devastating. None of the illustrations are fictional and all were shared with me in my counseling office. Most of these examples created feelings of rejection in the victim but were often not expressed until brought to the surface through counseling.

Although the list might seem exhaustive, it is by no means complete. I'm sure as you read and begin to understand the nature of **covert** rejection, you'll be able to add to the list from your own experience.

BIRTH

It Is Rejection When ...
- Mom had a difficult delivery and constantly reminds you how she went to death's door to give you life
- Your parents wanted a boy and you came instead
- Your parents wanted a girl, and you disappointed them
- You were conceived accidentally
- You were a late-in-life baby, and were expected to bring new joy to your parents' marriage
- The husband doesn't help the wife with the new baby
- A child is born with a birth defect
- A child is born out of wedlock
- A child is born to a single mother
- You are a twin and never get to celebrate your own birthday
- You are a twin and never get to wear your own clothes
- Premature birth separates the baby from its mother
- You were adopted at birth and had no bonding with your natural parents

CHILDHOOD

It Is Rejection When ...

- A child wears hand-me-downs all the time
- A child is called names such as dumb, stupid, brat, idiot (even in a kidding or teasing way)
- A child can't ever dress as nicely as other children
- A child must always wear the nicest clothes and keep perfectly clean
- A child is not allowed to be a child
- A child is never left with a babysitter or left alone
- A child is given the message, "I'll never leave you" and the parents divorce or die
- A child is told to "be seen and not heard"
- A child is given a nickname that makes fun of some physical problem (i.e., "Bucky" for buck teeth, "Chubs" for overweight, "Skinny" due to underweight)
- The oldest child has responsibility for the younger children
- The oldest child has to do all the work while the younger ones play
- A child is raised in extreme wealth or poverty
- A middle child is neglected
- The other children are neglected when the new baby arrives
- The youngest child is babied, pampered, and overprotected
- A child never gets hugged
- A child is given everything he wants
- A child is ten years old and Mom still combs his hair or picks out his clothes
- A child is expected to keep a perfectly neat room
- A child is allowed to be a slob and live in his own private pigpen
- A child is expected to act like an adult and behave as his parents' friends think he should
- One child is favored over the others

- A sickly child takes the parents' attention from the other children
- One child is compared to another sibling and hears, "Why can't you be like...?"
- A child is compared to other children outside the family
- A child never hears the words "I love you, I appreciate you, thank you"
- A child is given attention and praise based on performance only
- A child makes A's or B's and is not praised for that, but is criticized for the C
- A child is expected to excel in sports because his parents did
- A child is too short
- A child is too tall
- A child is expected to excel in academics, music or dance because his parents did
- A child is not allowed to make mistakes
- A child is told to get his schoolwork done so he can be a better person than his parents are
- A child is not allowed any choice in his dress style
- A child has no grandparents or can't spend time with grandparents
- A child has a learning disorder
- A child has a bedwetting problem
- A child has a sickness that he doesn't understand
- A child is picked last for a team

FAMILY

It Is Rejection When ...
- Mom and Dad are always fighting
- Mom and Dad never talk
- Mom and Dad start a fight in front of the kids, settle the argument in private, and don't let the kids know they've reconciled
- Parents criticize their mates in front of the kids

- Parents depend on young children and teenagers to help them solve their adult problems
- Dad never takes a vacation with the family
- Dad and Mom never attend school functions
- Dad and/or Mom are alcoholics
- Dad and/or Mom use drugs
- Dad and/or Mom are workaholics
- Dad and/or Mom always put the kids first and neglect themselves and each other
- Mom handles all the problems at school
- One parent does all the discipline
- The parent yells at the children
- The parent never spends time with the children individually
- Dad never laughs
- Mom never smiles
- Mom overprotects the children and won't let them make their own decisions
- One parent makes a child their confidante/surrogate spouse
- Relatives favor one child over another

ADOLESCENCE
It Is Rejection When ...
- A teenager has acne
- A teenager is not allowed to get his driver's license until he is 18 and most of his friends are driving at 16
- A teenager has to work long hours at a job and can't spend time with friends
- A teenager has no choice in style of dress
- A teenager acts as a parent to the younger children
- A teenager is not allowed to date at the same age as most other teens
- A teenager has a curfew which is unreasonable compared to that of his peers
- A teenager has no curfew

- A teenager has no privacy in his or her bedroom
- A teenager is not allowed to lock his bedroom door or the bathroom door
- A teenager's phone calls are monitored
- A teenager's belongings have been searched
- A teenager is never allowed to taste alcohol in family situations
- A teenager is allowed to drink or take drugs
- A teenager is under peer pressure to wear designer label or other trendy clothing
- A teenager is forced to work to help support the family
- A teenager is forced to have an abortion
- A teenager is forced to marry
- A young teenager dates an adult
- A teenager never dates
- A teenager is popular only because they are attractive or wealthy
- A teenager is rejected by peers for getting good grades
- Peers label a teenager with names like "jock", "nerd", and "narc"
- A teenager gets a new car and doesn't have to pay anything
- A teenager doesn't get a car
- A teenager isn't allowed to hold a part-time job to earn spending money
- A teenager can't find a job because he/she has no experience
- A teenager is not allowed to express opinions that differ from that of his parents
- Parents take custody of a teenager's out-of-wedlock child
- Parents criticize a teenager's choice in music and/or friends

SEX

It Is Rejection When ...
- Sex is never discussed in a healthy manner

- A girl starts her menstrual cycle and thinks she's bleeding to death
- A girl's first period is announced at the family dinner table
- A boy begins puberty and is teased about his pubic hair
- A girl begins puberty and is teased about her breasts
- A child perceives that sex is dirty
- A child develops prematurely and becomes the brunt of jokes from his/her peers
- A child comes out of puberty underdeveloped or overdeveloped
- A person gives sex to gain acceptance
- A child is molested or raped
- A person has been told that sex is wrong, but suddenly on his/her wedding night it is supposed to be perfectly fine
- A child is taught masturbation is a sin and evil
- A child is caught masturbating and the rest of the family is told
- A male never masturbates, particularly through the teen years
- Sex is withheld or used to bribe
- Nudity is never allowed on a casual level as the child develops
- Nudity is excessive and modesty is not taught
- The parents make crude comments with sexual overtones to the children
- One or both parents describe or discuss their sex life with the kids

MARRIAGE

It Is Rejection When ...

- A mate cannot have friends outside the marriage
- One mate tries to be the other's conscience
- One mate has too many friends or activities outside the marriage

- One mate is quiet and withdrawn
- One mate is demanding and hostile
- One mate is a workaholic and never spends time with the other mate
- One mate has an emotional affair
- One mate is addicted to pornography
- One mate uses masturbation to avoid intimacy with the other
- One mate criticizes the other in public
- One mate withholds affection and praise
- The words "I love you, appreciate you, thank you" are seldom used
- The in-laws move in
- Sex is used as a weapon
- Silence is used as a weapon
- One mate must always agree with the other mate
- The husband never calls the wife when he's away on business
- One mate is never allowed to "get away from it all" by himself/herself
- One mate is extremely possessive of the other
- There is no quiet time together except for sex
- The Lord is not the head of the family
- One mate praises other people, but not their mate

DIVORCE

It Is Rejection When ...

- One or both of your parents blames you for their divorce
- The children have to decide which parent with whom to spend the holidays
- You are criticized by one parent for taking the other parent's side
- The parent feels guilt for letting the children down
- Your divorce is blamed solely on you
- The mate wonders, "Did I do enough? Did I do everything possible?"

- The mate that leaves the children feels he/she has copped out
- The mate without the children realizes the other mate will ignore the children's needs
- The mate that leaves totally ignores the children's needs
- The mate that leaves never calls the children, forgets their birthdays, and makes promises which he/she doesn't keep
- The wife who has never worked outside the home, helped her husband get his education and build his career, suddenly becomes a non-human
- One spouse never had his/her name on credit cards and has no credit history
- The child support is always late or not paid

REMARRIAGE

It Is Rejection When ...

- A person withholds total commitment for fear of getting hurt again
- The children are considered a higher priority than the new mate
- The ex-spouse is considered a higher priority than the new mate
- A stepchild does not respond to the stepparent's authority and the natural parent sides with the child
- The natural parent defends the child's wrong behavior to the new stepparent
- The mate of a second marriage claims ownership of his/her material goods and feels they are not to be shared
- There is rivalry among the stepbrothers and stepsisters and you take your natural child's side
- There are activities for your stepchild, but none for you and your mate
- You spend more time and attention with, or otherwise favor, your natural children than with your stepchildren

- Your new mate complains about money spent on your natural child's needs
- Your new mate feels unwanted by your friends
- You feel unwanted by your new mate's old friends
- Your new mate feels unwanted by your parents
- You feel unwanted by your in-laws
- Your in-laws constantly bring up and compare you to the ex-spouse
- Your parents favor the natural grandchildren over the step-grandchildren
- Your new mate feels he/she cannot measure up to providing materially on the level of the previous mate
- Your ex-spouse finds ways to occupy your time and attention, causing hostility with your new mate
- Your ex-spouse acts seductively to you in front of your new spouse
- Your ex-spouse and you have sex
- Your new mate has a crippling habit that was hidden until after marriage
- A child of divorce has to readjust to his/her stepparent after spending time with the natural parent
- You defend or accept your ex-spouse's wrong behavior to your new mate out of fear of losing visitation or other legal battles
- Your new mate doesn't like your children; you don't like the new mate's children
- The non-custodial parent is late in picking up or visiting the kids, causing your schedule to be disrupted
- Your ex-spouse belittles you and/or your new mate to the kids
- You feel guilty about the divorce and are still emotionally tied to the ex-spouse
- A child is not allowed to love both the natural and stepparents at the same time

CAREER

It Is Rejection When ...

- You don't have a high school diploma
- You go to college just to please your parents
- You don't have a clue what career field you should pursue
- You are expected to be a doctor when you want to be a forest ranger
- You are doing what you enjoy most, but your parents wish you could have been more successful
- You are expected to carry on the family business when you have other goals you want to pursue
- You are seldom given words of praise or encouragement from your superior
- You seldom give words of praise or encouragement to your subordinates
- You are given more responsibility for the same pay
- You know you're at the top of the ladder with no chance of further promotion
- You know there is no future with your job
- You are in a position for which you are under or overqualified
- Your parents are always saying, "We're asking God to give you a better job."
- Others in the family with a better education or job put you down for where you are in life
- Success is measured primarily by how much money you earn
- You enjoy your job, but your mate wants you to change careers so you can make more money
- The mate who makes the most money reminds the other of it
- The wife who stays home with the children is made to feel less than successful
- You need to change career fields in mid-life but are fearful of the financial loss you may incur

- The wife tries to force her husband into early retirement

FINANCES

It Is Rejection When ...

- There is never enough money and the kids always hear about it
- Dad always gripes about how much money he spends on the family
- The wife works and her money is hers and the husband's money is his
- The bills are never paid
- One mate handles all the finances and the other is kept in the dark
- The wife criticizes her husband's ability to make money, or vice versa
- The kids never get any allowance
- The kids have to earn every dime their parents give them
- The parents give the kids everything and never expect them to earn money or be responsible for their needs
- A child has no say in how he/she spends his allowance
- A husband or wife has no say in how they spend their money
- A child is not taught money management at an early age
- A child has to account to the parents for every dime he spends
- The wife tries to make the husband tithe against his will
- The husband expects the wife to turn over her paycheck to him and she keeps nothing
- Parents help one child financially and not the others
- There's never enough money for the husband and wife to get away for the weekend or go out to dinner together
- The husband complains about the money he spends on his wife
- The wife complains she never has anything

- The wife works to provide for the family and the husband can't ever seem to get it together or find the right job
- You have to file bankruptcy

CHURCH

It Is Rejection When ...
- A person gets saved and is asked, "How do you feel now?" (He/she may not *feel* anything!)
- A person gets saved and is immediately told to prove their loyalty to the Lord
- A Christian is made to feel guilty for everything they do wrong (not everything wrong is a sin)
- A Christian's spirituality is measured by his outward actions
- A Christian is made to feel "backslidden" if he doesn't show up for every meeting
- A Christian feels stuck in a legalistic church
- A Christian is criticized for not participating in all church activities
- A Christian is criticized because he doesn't believe God wants him to be an officer or deacon, when the pastor has prayed about it and 'God told' the pastor to appoint the person
- A Christian is labeled as "not full of the Holy Ghost" if he doesn't speak in tongues
- A Christian's gift is not understood
- A person in the church disagrees with the leadership
- A Christian is made to feel insincere if he doesn't get baptized right away
- A Christian gets involved in church activities to gain acceptance
- One pastor's attendance is higher than another's
- Church involvement becomes an outside support system for a bad marriage

- Parents never spend a weekend away with the kids because they're always in church
- Legalism says you have to dress, talk, and act like the rest of the people in your church
- A Christian is made to feel inferior or inadequate if they don't attend the 'right' church or are of the 'right' denomination

Define **overt** rejection.

Define **covert** rejection.

Which is the most difficult to identify and why?

List three forms of covert rejection that you have experienced.

MENTAL MORSEL

*"The absence of a good thing is as destructive as
the presence of a bad thing."*

8

THE POVERTY SYNDROME

"I'll gladly pay you Tuesday for a hamburger today!" Didn't Popeye *ever* get tired of hearing Wimpy's pathetic plea for a loan?

We all know a friend who's always broke. Maybe it's someone with a good-paying job, but they're still always in debt. Worse yet, we may be *related* to them. We're frequently being hit up for a hamburger, but Tuesday never comes.

I'm not talking about the person who's temporarily laid off, or who can't find work because they've suffered a tragedy. This person to whom I refer is usually gainfully employed, hard working, and continually working to make ends meet. With every passing paycheck, though, those ends move further and further apart. It is painful hearing them bemoan the fact that they're always behind in their payments.

This person, like Popeye's friend, is caught up in the **Poverty Syndrome.** Like the proverbial puppy chasing its tail, this person can always see an end, but can never quite catch it.

How Much is Enough?
One day two men were talking and one asked the other, "How much *is* enough?"

"Just a little more," came the sarcastic reply. The old adage "the more you make the more you spend" is always true with a person caught in the **Poverty Syndrome**. It seems the cost of living continues to increase to meet their income.

The **Poverty Syndrome** affects a large percentage of our population and Christians are not excluded. It begins with a mental attitude. It's rooted in bitterness and is actually rejection recycling itself in the financial arena. Our attitude toward money and our ability to handle it are directly related to our mental and emotional stability or instability.

Here's a scary thought: only two out of every hundred Americans will be able to retire by age 65 without depending on an outside source for their financial needs! Even worse, fifty-three of those hundred retirees will be dependent on some form of government assistance. What about the remaining forty-five? Yep, you guessed it! They will be depending on their relatives to care for them.

Our nation, originally founded on principles of independence and freedom, has spawned a mass of financial bondage and dependency. Disgusting. *Depressing!*

What's happened? The Rejection Syndrome has produced, among other symptoms we've discussed, the **Poverty Syndrome.** *It's rejection of self* with debilitating financial attitudes and habits. Common examples include the following: "I'm not worth the better job"; "I'm not capable of handling money"; "I'm not disciplined enough to save money", or "I just can't take care of myself".

Are *you* caught up in the **Poverty Syndrome?**

Let's take a test to see if this is one of the symptoms of rejection in your life. Examples are given, followed with a scale of 0-10. Circle the appropriate number that you think most accurately represents the extent of the problem in your life. The '**0**' means *no improvement necessary* and the '**10**' means *improvement critically needed.*

78

Symptom 1 - Irresponsible Spending
Purchasing goods on impulse - not need. Buying it because
it's on sale at 10% off if you open a charge account. With
interest compounded from 14-22% annually, the 10%
discount really gets lost in the (shopping) bag! Often our
final cost, after months and months of payments, is over
300% the original price! Oh, but we're smart shoppers! It's
easy to see why the clerk *smiles* when she asks you "Cash or
CHARGE?"

One of the latest gimmicks in merchandising is the credit
card that pays you back 1% of your purchases. You charge
$1,000 and get $10 back at the end of the year. Whoopee!
What about the *$150 - $200 you pay in interest* just in the
first year of payments?? Impulse spenders are lured by pretty
packaging, fun fads, or savvy styles. The out-of-control
spending is a testimony to their insecurity. They are
spending frantically to buy the gift they most need: peace
with themselves.
Circle One: 0 1 2 3 4 5 6 7 8 9 10

Symptom Two - Low Self Esteem
A person's self esteem is evidenced in the way he or she
handles money. One who dislikes self can't consciously
allow self to stabilize financially. Recreating financial stress
becomes another habit for some Rejection Junkies. One way
to avoid spending money on someone you resent is to make
sure you have no money to spend. Stay in debt. Simple
routine. Being broke is miserable, but familiar. It's self-
inflicted punishment (rejection). It reminds you of your
worthlessness and keeps you feeling so.
Circle One: 0 1 2 3 4 5 6 7 8 9 10

Symptom Three - Self Pity
Poor me! I've never had anything in life. I've never been
given the right break. If only my parents had been wealthy.
If only I could win the lottery. I never had a good education.

It's the IRS, they did it to me! My brother got all the breaks! *Poor, poor me!*

The most depressing part of this familiar song is the singer truly believes he/she has been a victim of circumstances. Well, he'd be singing the same tune in just a matter of time even if he *did* win the lottery! "The IRS took most of it in taxes (poor me!) I had to help my parents! My kids bled me to death! My business failed! My partner was crooked!" Wahh-wahh-wahh! Enough said.

Circle One: 0 1 2 3 4 5 6 7 8 9 10

Symptom Four - Misplaced Blame
Similar to self pity, but a little more respectable on the surface, misplaced blame is very believable. The person fitting this description has a well-considered opinion of why he or she is where they are and whose fault it is. It's *never* their fault. As long as this person lays blame outside himself, he never has to really deal with his own attitudes or problems. Have you heard these familiar lines?

My parents didn't teach me.
My parents didn't help me.
My brother didn't guide me.
My wife didn't follow me.
My children didn't listen.
My company doesn't appreciate me.
And last, but not least, *God didn't bless me!*

Circle One: 0 1 2 3 4 5 6 7 8 9 10

Symptom Five - Undue Criticism
Have you heard someone constantly complain the sun is too bright, the moon too round? The kids are too loud, the dessert is too sweet, the rain is too wet, and the night is too dark? You name it, everything is just *too* something! When it comes to other people in this person's life, they're too greedy, too demanding, *even too happy.* This person finds fault in everyone and everything. It's no surprise his critical

spirit also infects his financial situation. Although he may be criticizing others for why they don't deserve what they earn, or how easy it came to them, or how poorly they spend their money, he is covering up for his own financial mess. He's trying to hide the fact he hasn't, can't or won't ever earn it, and doesn't get to spend it. He can't, he won't, and he'll never own it. By diverting the attention to others, he doesn't have to admit he's a financial failure himself. Day after day his criticism of others helps him justify his own miserable lot in life, at least to himself.

Circle One: 0 1 2 3 4 5 6 7 8 9 10

Symptom Six - Guilt For Success

This poor guy goes on so many guilt trips, he's never home! If someone gave him a million dollars he'd feel guilty. He'd feel guilty for driving a new car, owning his own home, or having a savings account. He can't go on vacations or wear new clothes without guilt. You name it, if it has to do with taking care of himself or making himself comfortable, he'd feel guilty. Why? Usually in his background he heard verbal or nonverbal messages such as:

" You'll never have anything.
Never take God's blessings for granted because you
     could lose them tomorrow.
Don't be greedy and ask God for more than you need.
You'll never amount to anything.
Remember, people are starving all over the world! **"**

As other people's guilt is heaped on him, he goes through life feeling unworthy of the good things that come his way. He takes and carries guilt which is not his own. What happens then? He becomes a victim of the **Poverty Syndrome,** and unconsciously fulfills the prophecy of "You'll never amount to anything."

Circle One: 0 1 2 3 4 5 6 7 8 9 10

Symptom Seven - The Financial Rescuer

This person believes it's his responsibility (often his *Christian* duty) to rescue others from financial dilemmas. The most common rescuer is the parent playing the role of "the goose that laid the golden egg." He deprives his children of the chance to learn financial independence. The financially dependent children embark towards adulthood with vice grips on Mom's and Dad's purse strings - often with the attitude of entitlement. Many people whom I've counseled who were fifty or older were still financially dependent on their aging parents. Some parents in their 60's and 70's face bankruptcy to bail out their adult children who go from one crisis to another. *The financial rescuers are paying a hefty ransom to gain what little acceptance their adult children give them!*

"My children will reject me"; "My friends will criticize me for being too tough"; "God blessed me with money, I should share with those less fortunate"; "What Father gives his son stones when he asks for bread?" Yes, financial rescuers can quote and misinterpret scriptures with the best of them!

Sadly, those being rescued are resentful because they feel they've been forced to be dependent in the first place. It's a dead end road for all concerned. Financial rescuers need to pay heed to the old adage, "Give a man a fish and you feed him for a day. Teach him to fish and he'll eat for the rest of his life." *When you don't rescue, others are allowed to fail.* Their opportunity to learn from failing can be the greatest gift of all.

Circle One: 0 1 2 3 4 5 6 7 8 9 10

Symptom Eight - Buying Friendships

This person never goes to lunch without picking up the tab and never goes to visit friends or relatives without bearing gifts. What he is actually saying is "I'm so insecure that I want to do something (perform) extra to assure you'll like and accept me." The Buyer of Friendship is close kin to the Financial Rescuer. The difference is that relationships with the beneficiary are short term. The Buyer of Friendship may frequently change friends as often as he changes clothes. Why? When the extra efforts are not being returned by similar favors, he rejects that friend and starts the search for another on whom to bestow his generosity! Once discovered, this person is marked and mocked by others as being manipulative and controlling. Caught in the cycle of rejecting and being rejected, the Buyer of Friendship is a **Rejection Junkie** in full bloom!

Circle One: 0   1   2   3   4   5   6   7   8   9   10

Scoring Your Test
There is a multitude of other symptoms associated with being caught in the **Poverty Syndrome**: lack of investments, late payments of monthly bills, living on credit, habitual gambling, crisis creation, envy of what others have, just to name a few.

Add the score on the eight symptoms. If you score 40 or more, you're in the **Poverty Syndrome,** probably convinced you can't change your financial situation. You became programmed to fail financially when you heard some things like:

- ✓ Your parents never made it, so chances are that you won't make it either
- ✓ You can't be wealthy and serve the Lord
- ✓ The Bible says that it is sinful to have money or financial security
- ✓ Money is the root of all evil
- ✓ Do not lay up treasures for yourself on earth
- ✓ Don't let your right hand know what your left hand is doing

Is there a way out? Yes! You can escape the **Poverty Syndrome** but you must first change your attitude toward money.

What the Bible Really Tells Us About Money

Actually the Bible says, "For the *love* of money is the root of all evil." I Timothy 6:10. Did you know it is possible to teach anything to be scriptural if you twist it enough? We could even teach that it's scriptural to commit suicide. The Bible says "Judas went and hanged himself." Then the Bible tells us, "Whatsoever thou doest, do quickly." Are we really to go and do likewise?

Don't let anyone misuse scripture to keep you in financial bondage. Money is a very useful tool and should be respected as such.

Money can cheer you up. "A feast is made for laughter and wine maketh merry, but *money answers all things.*" Ecclesiastes 10:19. Wow! What a statement!

Wouldn't you rather go to the store *with* money than *without* money? It's fun to go shopping and it is **not wrong to have money**. What can be wrong is our attitude toward money.

The real tragedy strikes when a person loses what God has given him because he didn't learn to manage what he had. Read the story in Matthew 25:15-18. It's a heartbreaking story of a man caught in the **Poverty Syndrome**. His problem was fear. He took the talent his lord had given him and buried it in the ground. When his lord returned and required an explanation of how he invested his talent, the man said "I was afraid and went and hid the talent in the earth." That is such a sad statement. He didn't manage what he had for fear of losing it. His real fear was that if he did lose it, he'd be rejected. There were Rejection Junkies in the New Testament!

84

Well, the poor guy lost it anyway. His lord said, "Take therefore the talent from him and give it unto him which hath ten talents. For unto everyone that hath shall be given, and he shall have abundance: but from him that hath not shall be taken away *even that which he hath.*" Matthew 25:28-29.

How Do You Manage Your Money?
People in the Poverty Syndrome follow the same pattern. They lose what they have, and then complain about those who have it. There are three types of money managers. Which type are you?

1) Water Treaders
You have been, and are still, treading water in your financial life. You never go under, but neither do you get up and get out of your situation.

2) Thinkers and Sinkers
Pretend you're in a boat in the middle of a lake and you just sprung a leak. As the boat starts sinking, you start thinking about what to do. Should I yell for help? Should I start rowing for shore? Should I start bailing out the water? *While you're thinking, you're sinking!*

3) Row-and-Go Gang
These people are the ones who recognize the emergency. They know that change is needed immediately and start rowing for safety. And they make it!

If you haven't already decided to join the Row-and-Go Gang yet, consider ...

The Man in the Glass

When you get what you want in your struggle
    for self,
And the world makes you king for a day,

Just go to the mirror and look at yourself,
And see what that man has to say.

For it isn't your father, mother or wife
Whose judgment upon you must pass,
The fellow whose verdict counts most in your life
Is the one staring back from the glass.

Some people may think you're a straight-shooting
    chum,
And call you a wonderful guy,
But the man in the glass says you're only a bum
If you can't look him straight in the eye.

He's the fellow to please - never mind all the rest
For he's with you clear up to the end,
And you've passed your most dangerous,
    difficult test,
If the man in the glass is your friend.

You may fool the whole world down the pathway
    of life
And get pats on your back as you pass,
But your final reward will be heartaches and tears,
If you've cheated the man in the glass!

- Author Unknown

List the symptoms of the Poverty Syndrome with which you identify.

What does the Bible *really* say about money?

Name the three types of money managers.

MENTAL MORSEL

"A person's ability to make and manage money is directly related to his emotional stability or instability."

9

THE FAILURE SYNDROME

Steve was handsome and intelligent, with a charismatic personality. A graduate of Bible college and seminary, he'd been the pastor of a church in Southern New Mexico. Under Steve's leadership for the last seven years, the church had experienced phenomenal growth. Steve had achieved national recognition in his denomination and was a celebrated motivational speaker.

Sadly, Steve, now in his mid-thirties, was sitting in my counseling office, pouring out his story of recent heartbreak and failure. His pastoral career had come to a screeching halt. His wife had filed for divorce and moved with the children to another state. His reputation lay in ruin and he was facing bankruptcy.

In the privacy of the counseling office, Steve was ablaze with emotions of anger, guilt, depression and self-condemnation. Although he'd valiantly fought and won many battles, he was losing the war.

Steve had an affair with a woman in his church. When discovered, the affair had become the final nail in his coffin of self-sabotage. Steve's wife could not face the humiliation nor handle the betrayal of his unfaithfulness. His story unfolded through spasms of sobbing and immense pain. His reasoning was distorted. Steve blamed not only himself but everyone and everything else.

In a quiet moment, he took a deep breath, relaxed a little and declared, "I'm a failure. I've failed at everything I've tried to do."

Two of Steve's statements punctuated his emotional condition: "I guess the Lord never intended for me to be successful", and "I hate to admit it, I'm just like my Dad". Sound familiar?

The self-sabotage of relationships and careers is commonplace among Rejection Junkies. Caught up in the Poverty Syndrome, Steve was a Rejection Junkie on the fast track to failure.

Failure and Poverty - Rooted in Bitterness
The root of bitterness gives birth to both the Poverty Syndrome and the Failure Syndrome that stems from it. The same principles of pollination, that process which gives life to plants, apply to these syndromes. Pollination occurs from one plant to another, from within a single flower, or from one blossom to another. The Failure Syndrome is the result of pollination from many other symptoms, including:

Poor self image	Laziness
Dishonesty	Fear of rejection
Perfectionism	Indecisiveness
Unrealistic goal setting	Lack of goal setting
Hyper-spiritualism	Analyzing and paralyzing

And the list could go on. We know these surface symptoms are only a testimony of a deeper conflict.

We also know that God uses many methods to pollinate plant life. Bees, birds, animals, wind, and water each carry pollen to plants. Like these elements, the bitterness syndromes help perpetuate each other. As two blooms rooted in bitterness, the Poverty and Failure Syndromes continue to cross-pollinate until every last ounce of hope and a chance for survival has been sucked from their victim. Caught in a whirlwind of self-destruction, the victims of the Failure

90

Syndrome eventually lose control. The debris of broken dreams and lost hopes litters their lives.

Winds and Waters of Destruction

These elements which pollinate also decimate. There was a time in my life when the waters of self-destruction had thrashed my soul onto the rocks of despair. The winds of self-hatred had destroyed the foundations of decency and morality in my life.

I'm reminded of the time Jesus went sailing in a crude wooden ship with his friends. Under the clear skies, Jesus had drifted off to sleep. The storm, which had crept in slowly, was now raging ferociously and the boat was quickly flooding. The disciples feared for their lives, but Jesus still slept.

"And they came to Him, and awoke Him, saying, 'Master, Master, we perish'. Then he arose and rebuked the wind and the raging of the water: and they ceased, and there was a calm." Luke 8:24.

The reason you're reading this book is probably that there's a massive storm in your life. Are there tidal waves of fear, hurt, shame, or hopelessness? Have hurricanes of failure blown into your life? You may feel that your ship is sinking, that God is sleeping and doesn't hear *your* cries.

Many Christians are frustrated, even angry, that they've cried to the Lord for help, but their circumstances haven't calmed down. Perhaps things have continued to get worse.

Stop and think on this for a moment:

Sometimes God calms the storm.
Sometimes God lets the storm rage
while He calms His child.

Is there safety for you? Is there escape to safe harbor? Yes! But, if you find peace only when the winds are calm and the waters are still, you're focusing on the *situation* and not the *Savior*.

God says, "Who hath ascended up into heaven or descended? Who hath gathered the wind in His fists? Who hath bound the waters in a garment? Who hath established all the ends of the earth? What is His name, and what is His son's name, if thou canst tell? Every word of God is pure; He is a shield unto them that put their trust in Him." Proverbs 30:4-5.

A Rejection Junkie whose life is caught in the Failure Syndrome needs to understand this truth:

> ***While God can gather the wind in His fists,***
> ***He can also protect you.***

The Secret to Success
Steve felt God had abandoned him. Even his recent heavy drinking couldn't help him escape the pain. Now he was alone with me in my office.

After the long emptying of his soul's stored-up anguish, Steve became quiet - almost numb.

I got up from behind my desk and sat in the empty chair next to Steve. I put my hand on his shoulder and assured him that in our counseling, we do not judge or condemn anyone for their behavior. I explained we all have dark shadows in our past. My staff and I never place ourselves above our clients. We are *all the same*.

Steve seemed surprised when I told him I'd had similar problems in my past. No one is above failing. Consider I Corinthians 10:13: "There hath no temptation taken you but such as is common to man: but God is faithful, who will not suffer you to be tempted above that which ye are able; but will with the temptation also make a way to escape, that ye may be able to bear it."

I asked Steve why he'd chosen me as his counselor. He responded that he'd been listening to our radio broadcast for several years. He added, "If I'd come in when I first heard you, I wouldn't be in this mess."

I replied, "Steve, let me tell you the *real* reason you chose me. It's not because I'm a good counselor, not because I'm on the radio, and certainly not because I have all the answers!"

"The only reason you chose me is because I have failed. I have failed as a husband, as a father, and I have failed financially. I have faced bankruptcy twice. I have failed in many, many ways, but as *a result of failing I now have success.*"

"Steve," I asked, "what would you be willing to give for the secret of success?"

"I'd give anything, if I knew it would work," came his reply.

I handed Steve a pen and writing tablet. "Listen carefully," I cautioned, "and write down what I have come to know as the *only* secret to success."

The Secret to Success
"If I want to succeed, all I have to do is fail. Fail again and fail some more. Fail, then fail again and fail some more. Then fail, and fail, and fail and fail, and fail and fail, and fail, and then fail some more."

"Then keep on failing until success breaks through! I am not a failure because I have failed. I can only be a failure if I allow failing to become the last chapter of the book I'm writing."

"Have you failed?" I asked Steve. "Yes," he answered.

"Are you a failure?" I asked.

He hesitated, then answered "Yes."

"Read it again, Steve," I advised. "Read it aloud."

As Steve read word by word, his expression began to change. Then he read the last sentence, "I can only be a failure if I allow failing to become the last chapter of the book I am writing."

I asked, "Have you written the last chapter of your book?" "No!" he insisted. "Have you failed?" "Yes!" he retorted.

"Are you a failure, Steve?"

He was quiet.

I pressed again with the question "Are you a failure?" After a moment, a wry grin crossed his mouth. With a little relief and a lot of conviction he replied, "No, I'm not a failure, but I sure have screwed up!"

There was new resolve, a hint of hope in his voice, as he continued, "I've not written the last chapter of the book I'm writing, but I doubt if anyone would want to publish it anyway!"

We both laughed. How exciting! Here was a man who was just starting to realize he was like the rest of the human race and it wasn't the end of the world. Steve came to understand that each and every failing experience was another step toward success!

Can a Rejection Junkie break free from the Failure Syndrome? Yes!

In Chapter 17, **"The Emotional Surgery"**, we'll tell you how. But for now, understand that everything that takes place in the Failure Syndrome is nothing more than behavior symptoms given birth by the root of bitterness.

List five symptoms of the Failure Syndrome with which you identify.

What is the secret to success?

When do we become failures?

Mental Morsel

"Sometimes God calms the storm: sometimes God lets the storm rage, while He calms His child."

10

PASSPORT TO PERFORMANCE

Hurry! In a few minutes the bus will leave. We're taking a trip through the **Land of Performance**. Since we were all born and raised there, it will be good as fellow countrymen to visit the various villages of our origin.

All aboard, **Rejection Junkies!** Everyone who's ever been made to perform at certain levels for fear of rejection is welcome. All but one, that is. The only fellow we don't want on our trip is *Positive Self Image*. We **Rejection Junkies** don't like being around him because we just can't attain the joyful life he offers. Since his positive attitude will just ruin our trip, let's leave him behind.

Parental Acceptance
Our first stop is just around the bend at the **Village of Parental Acceptance**. This little hamlet is named after every Rejection Junkie's first desire. Do you recognize these streets? As children we learned here that our value in life was, for the most part, based on *what we do,* not *who we are.* Here we earned our parents' pleasure and affirmation by our behavior. If we were bad, we were treated with displeasure and disappointment. Although it was good to be taught how to behave, most of us never received a true understanding of our value as a person. Maybe we never heard the words, "I love you", "I appreciate you", or "I accept you as you are". Our parents, also Rejection Junkies, usually didn't have the time or knowledge to meet *our* emotional needs. Their parents probably rejected *them.*

We don't blame Mom and Dad; they did the best they could. However, understanding the destructive force of rejection helps us see how we became the people we are. With so much rejection, we never learn to love ourselves the way God loves us. It was Mom and Dad who were our 'god' and even today we have difficulty separating our parents' opinion of us from that of our Heavenly Father's. As we travel through Performance, we still seek our parents' acceptance.

Sibling Rivalry

The next village along our route was a place of many tears, a frustrating town where some of us often felt alone, worthless, and even hopeless. When I lived here, I learned I could never make the grade in life. See it ahead? Down at the bottom of the road? It's **The Village of Sibling Rivalry**.

Our brothers and sisters often recycled to us the same rejection they'd been getting. To them we were just 'dummies' or 'stupid'. Did your siblings call you 'four eyes' because you wore glasses, or "Dumbo" because you had big ears? Maybe you were the tag-along - always in their way. As the youngest of three boys, I wanted so badly to be just like my big brothers. And what about my sister? Well, she was okay but she was 'just a girl'.

The strange thing about sibling rivalry is that everything is usually very exaggerated:
They were always right...I was always wrong.
They were very smart...I was very stupid.
They were super-strong...I was pathetically weak.
They were handsome princes...I was the ugly frog.
They were the athletes...I was the water boy!

Adulthood seemed so far away! I wondered if I'd ever survive all the rejection my siblings dumped on me.

I didn't realize, though, that I was beginning to get addicted to their rejection. Addicted? *Their rejection meant attention,*

98

even if it was negative. If they left me alone, I'd come up with something to get them to reject me. I was a little kid looking for a fix of rejection from my big brothers.

Just as I'd vowed in my heart to someday be "just like" them, I did become like my brothers. I was troubled and defiled by the root of bitterness. As we visit this village, can you see that we may be more like our siblings than we care to admit? They were addicted to rejection; why should we be any different?

Typically, most adult siblings still live in performance and have adult relationships with each other that are as fractured as they were when they were children. The *past* bitterness still has a vice grip on the *present.*

Peer Pressure
Next we visit a very confusing community. The town of **Peer Pressure** is where we lost all identity and sense of individuality. Feeling unloved and unwanted by parents and siblings, many of us turned to our peers. To gain their acceptance, our behavior and even our manner of dress began to change drastically. We didn't know it then, but our peers were feeling just as insecure and rejected as we were. Lots of little Rejection Junkies, trying so hard to be something they weren't with others who didn't know what or who *they* were! In the **Land of Performance**, chaos spread nationwide.

It was the 1950's and I performed well. I smoked and drank. My flattop haircut gave way to the greased-back look with a 'duck bill' hanging down in the middle of my forehead. I traded my bicycle in for a green, 1947 two-door Plymouth coupe I called 'The Green Bean'. Sporting the all-occasion outfit of a white tee-shirt, pegged pants, and roach-killer pointed shoes, I graduated from the skating rink to the dance floor where, in my junior year, I won the best dancer award.

Oh, was I so cool! With my cigarettes rolled up in my tee-shirt sleeve, I hung out with the other Rejection Junkies, playing poker, shootin' pool and dealin' a mean game of Black Jack. The chicks were cute, and we'd 'get with it', 'get it on', 'neck', and 'make out'.

Hormones raging and high on life, I even stole a police cruiser one night! Hoping to be noticed, I turned the school parking lot into a racetrack using flashing lights and wailing sirens. I was noticed, all right! Unfortunately, it was by another police car parked across the street.

As suddenly as it had come, it was over. Toward the end of my senior year, as things quieted down, I heard unfamiliar music. It was a weird and strange song they hadn't played at our parties called *"Pomp and Circumstance"*. It was High School graduation! What was I doing there?

Can you take a minute and recall your own foolish behavior during those years? Sometimes that walk down memory lane is embarrassing, isn't it? You see, when you live in the **Land of Performance**, you become willing to tap dance on any table top to gain a little acceptance. Before we leave the town of **Peer Pressure** for the next stop, I'd like to share this poem I wrote in dedication to all Rejection Junkies:

The Tap Dancer

Tap dancing on the table tops
Of other people's lives,
A Rejection Junkie's 'Performance Trip',
That's how he thrives.

He says:

"Let me entertain you,
Let me be your friend,

100

Let me prove to all of you
That liking me is 'in'.

I can do the shuffle,
I can do the swing,
I'll do the boogie-woogie
And, for you, I'll even sing!

I'll go for you, I'll do for you
Anything you want,
I just need to gain acceptance,
How's *that* for being blunt?

I'm insecure, that's for sure,
My life is full of strife.
I'm so busy dancing for you,
I don't even have a life.

My mother doesn't like me,
My father even less,
My brothers and my sisters
And, even me, I guess.

Dancing on your table top
Takes a lot of skill.
Having poor self-image,
Takes a lot of will.

A *Rejection Junkie's* life style
Demands a daily fix.
Just to gain acceptance,
I'll do many tricks.

What's my value, who am I?
I really don't give a 'rip'.
I'm just a Rejection Junkie
On a big 'Performance Trip'.

A Little Town Called College Bound
Some of us, forced by our parents, had to move to the town of **College Bound**. To be successful, said society, we had to go to college. So, all the 'smart' people went to college and the 'dummies' took jobs in the local factories. Sad thing, though, a lot of us who went to college found ourselves rejected again by our parents (if we didn't have the right major), by our professors (if we didn't make the grade), or by our peers (if we didn't party with the right group).

I remember some of my buddies who came home half way through college were labeled as 'drop outs' and viewed as failures. Even those who did graduate from college often got stuck in careers their parents had chosen. (Sadly, over 90% of all professionals eventually find themselves in a career field they never studied for in the first place!) We *went where* and *did what* others told us and eventually found we were **miserable**.

Career City
Are you enjoying our trip? As our bus rambles up the next bend, we find **Career City** right past **College Bound**. This village was more like a bustling metropolis once we found ourselves performing in our careers. Did we end up doing what our parents wanted? Did we feel we owed them because they paid our tuition? Didn't we want to perform where Mom and Dad advised all the money is? How many of us were rejected as rebels if we dared to follow our philosophical instincts and sacrifice wealth for a worthy cause?

A lot of us did settle for the money. Hey, if we're going to be miserable, we might as well be miserable in comfort! We told ourselves that maybe the rejection would stop if we were successful in our career. Unfortunately, most of us have found that rejection never goes away and is in *every* career.

What about our reputation? The concern you had for your reputation in high school is nothing compared to the worries about your reputation in your career. Many lives and reputations have been shipwrecked in the name of 'building a successful career'. Spouses, children, home life, and even physical health are the prices we're willing to pay to gain our bosses' or clients' acceptance. We're doomed to a miserable existence in this crowded, noisy place until, maybe, we can move to the **Village of Retirement**.

Village of Retirement (Home of the not-so Golden Oldies)
Dreaming of a cute little condo or traveling around the land in their RV, the senior citizens of the **Land of Performance** anticipate glorious relief from the years and years of **Past Performance**. Unfortunately, most retirees who make it to this village are still full-blown Rejection Junkies and they are too tired, too broke, and too bitter to enjoy their Golden Years. Performing for others has left most retirees with no energy to develop their own interests, much less the finances. Victims of the Poverty or Failure Syndromes, the aging citizens of **Performance Land** never reach the Promised Land.

Bitter because their children never come to see them, or angry that their now-retired spouse sits around with nothing to do, the senior citizens are nothing like those gray-haired couples whistling and riding bikes in the Geritol commercials. For maybe the first time in their lives, these folks will wish too late that they'd gotten off the bus and taken a trip through some other country than the **Land of Performance.**

The Emerald City of Christianity
Have you noticed the sparkling towers in the distance as we've traveled through the **Land of Performance**? See? At the end of the road? They're up on the highest hill, visible from all four corners of the land. Life there is promised to be

wonderful, a reward for all our years of performance, where we'll enjoy "life and life more abundantly". Citizens live in contentment and tranquillity and even the streets are named Love, Joy, Peace, Longsuffering, Gentleness, Goodness, Faith, Meekness, and Temperance. The road signs promise grace, acceptance, and God's unconditional love when we enter this wonderful **Village of Christianity**.

Wait a minute! What's Christianity doing in the **Land of Performance**? Did we get on the wrong bus? Has our driver taken a wrong turn? Christianity doesn't belong in performance ... and, folks, *performance doesn't belong in Christianity!*

God's church is filled with people and, like you and me, they all were - or are - *Rejection Junkies.* Where there are Rejection Junkies there *will* be rejection, even in the church. How else would they feed their habit?

The Three Brothers
Every village has its notorious citizens like Mayberry's town drunk, Otis Campbell. In the **Village of Christianity**, there are three brothers who create havoc wherever they go. The oldest brother is *False Guilt,* a tyrannical fellow who loves to make you squirm. Most Christians live with False Guilt because they fear others will reject them.

> *False Guilt is anxiety created from a fear*
> *of being rejected for lack of performance.*

False Guilt terrorizes and paralyzes even the most sincere Christian. He will cause you to spend your days in agony worrying over how you can better perform to please others. When new converts move to the **Village of Christianity**, False Guilt will exhort them to start 'living for the Lord'. When you've heard this brother preach, he says something like this:

"Now that you're saved, you need to ... (perform)"
"If you really love the Lord, you will ... (perform)"
"If you care for others, you should ... (perform)"

What False Guilt's message really says is, "If you perform for us, we'll accept you. If you don't, we'll reject you."

Many Christians trade the burden of sin
for the burden of righteousness.

They haven't learned that *peace* comes from our *position* in Christ, not our *performance* for Him. They haven't learned that "...He hath made us accepted in the Beloved." Ephesians 1:6.

They haven't learned that "... there is therefore now no condemnation to them which are in Christ Jesus." Romans 8:1. They haven't learned that "being justified by faith, we have peace with God through our Lord Jesus Christ." Romans 5:1.

Genuine Guilt is the Holy Spirit's gift to us. He understands our hearts and will minister to us without the condemnation of False Guilt.

Genuine Guilt is grieving
created by the Holy Spirit over a situation.

Whew! I am so glad I stopped 'living for the Lord'! Say what? I am truly glad I stopped tap dancing on God's table, because ...

Pious Christians live for the Lord.
Spirit-controlled Christians
let the Lord live through them.

105

When a Christian focuses on his or her *position in Christ* and not their *performance for Christ*, you can be sure others will reject them.

Another of the dastardly brothers is **Legalism.** He is a deadly enemy of Grace.

Legalism says:
Perform so you can gain acceptance.

Grace says:
You are accepted, now you can perform.

Legalism makes man's preference equal to God's Word. He preaches that if you don't dress, act, pray, or think just like he does, you are not really a Christian. Legalism is the Captain of Bondage, choking the life out of churches and bringing Christians to their knees in defeat.

Legalism condemns you. Grace **forgives** you. Legalism oppresses you. Graces **frees** you.

God's grace is a message of acceptance, not rejection. Rejection Junkies are frustrated with Grace because they think they need rejection. Remember, Paul wrote, "I do not frustrate the grace of God: for if righteousness comes by the law, then Christ is dead in vain." Galatians 2:21.

Unlike False Guilt and Legalism, the third brother is more of a town nuisance than a threat. His name is *Religious Activity.* He keeps the citizens of Christianity busy praying, witnessing, going to church, attending prayer meetings, missionary meetings, board meetings, and reading the Bible until they go blind! Then Religious Activity tells the poor people to memorize Scripture, teach Sunday schools, sing in the choir, and join the praise and worship team!

I counseled a fellow who was simultaneously serving on fourteen boards of directors! That's not faith, that's foolishness!

Some Christians are so busy performing, they have no time to fellowship with Christianity's founding Father and His Son, the Lord Jesus Christ.

Religious activity has never produced spiritual maturity.

SPIRITUAL MATURITY:
A matter of what God does for you,
***not* what you do for Him.**

A Journey Ended
Well, folks, our trip through the **Land of Performance** is over. I'm sure you're all tired just *thinking* about all that performance. In a few moments we'll be stopping at the station and hopefully many of you will decide to really 'get off the bus' this time.

I've written another poem as a good-bye present. I hope you enjoyed the trip!

The Empty Table Top

Perched loftily on tabletops
of other people's lives,
A true Rejection Junkie,
I believed so many lies.

Now I Say;
I used to entertain you,
I tried to be your friend,
I wanted so to prove to you
That liking me was 'in'.

I bragged about my dancing,
Of my skill I was proud.
At the throne of man's acceptance,
On my knees you'd find me bowed.

I went for you, I did for you,
Whatever you desired.
I needed man's acceptance,
But now I'm very tired.

So insecure, that's for sure,
My life was full of strife.
Tapping, twirling just for you,
I didn't have a life.

Most people didn't like me,
I felt faceless in the crowd.
But when I learned the grace of God
could heal, I cried aloud:

"Oh Lord, have mercy on me,
My weary soul set free!
Remove my poor self-image,
Conform me, now, to Thee!"

Dancing on those tabletops,
had taken lots of skill.
But loving me as Jesus does,
That is my Father's will.

Acceptance, not rejection,
For that I'd truly yearned.
But God bestowed his grace on me,
And this is what I learned:

The Spirit's gifts of love, joy, peace,
Blessed fruits they are,

They don't just cover up the pain,
But heal, remove the scar.

The tabletop's now empty.
At last I'm off the stage.
No longer needing man's acclaim,
My life has turned the page.

Someone else, turn out the lights!
The entertainer has gone home.
He's left Performance Land for good,
Never more to roam.

One last message to our travelers: you don't have to stay on the bus. You can get off any time you want and begin to enjoy the life God has prepared for you. Consider this book a travel brochure for a much more satisfying destination: *Mental and Emotional Freedom*!

List the Villages of Performance in which you have lived.

Name the three Dastardly Brothers who live in the Village of Christianity.

Define *False Guilt.*

Define *Genuine Guilt.*

MENTAL MORSEL

*"Peace comes from our position in Christ,
not our performance for Christ."*

11

EMOTIONAL ENERGY THIEVES

Picture yourself strapped in a chair. As you look down you can see and feel hundreds of long, black electrical cords plugged into your arms, legs, your body, and into the sides and top of your head. You can almost hear the low, pulsating sound of those cords as they suck the strength and energy out of your body. You feel weak, tired and trapped. Twisting and squirming, you try to break free. You want to scream, to rip those cords out, but you can't. Hopeless, you begin to cry.

All **Rejection Junkies** are connected to their past and controlled in the present by the emotional cords of bitterness. At the ends of the cords are all the people and circumstances of their past. As long as they're 'plugged in' to you, the cords of bitterness will continue to steal your emotional energy, peace, serenity, and joy.

The Puppet Masters
Emotional energy thieves are like puppet masters. They pull the strings that make you jump, dance and perform. As the entertaining marionette, you are at their mercy. Through your own bitterness, control of your life has been given to the puppet master of your choice.

To determine who or what has become an 'Emotional Energy Thief' to you, ask yourself, "Does this person, thing, or circumstance create one or more of the following responses within me?"

✤ An inward resentment	✤ An anxiety
✤ An avoidance	✤ A wounded spirit
✤ A sense of abandonment	✤ A guilt
✤ A sense of betrayal	✤ A fear

111

If you recognize one or more of these mental or emotional responses, you've identified an 'Emotional Energy Thief' in your life. Following are some more examples of common ones:

Relatives
Parents, grandparents, step-parents, spouses, ex-spouses, children, step-children, brothers, sisters, step-brothers, step-sisters, aunts, uncles, cousins, mothers and fathers-in law, brothers and sisters-in-law. Any of the above that may be deceased.

Careers
Previous and present employers, subordinates, supervisors, co-workers, competitors, companies, businesses, broken promises and dreams of success in any given field, teachers, counselors, or students.

Cultures
Certain races or nationalities of people, personality types, body types, ages, dress styles, social ethics, political morays or movements, government agencies, and ethnic demands.

Finances
Money or the inability to make money, bad investments or people who have taken advantage of you financially, material goods such as houses, property, vehicles, estates, wills, investment funds, retirement funds, etc. (It's amazing how much emotional energy is invested in financial matters!)

Religion
Churches, denominations, and beliefs, people who choose those denominations or beliefs, preachers, priests, deacons and nuns, any person who had a

negative effect in your religious life, any religious experience which has caused bitterness in your soul.

Miscellaneous
Health problems, loss of bodily functions such as sight, speech, hearing and walking, addictive habits, body shape or size, food, sex, nudity, lovemaking, friends and friendships, neighbors, and your precious reputation.

The list of Emotional Energy Thieves could be never-ending. If you're honest, you'll discover many are plugged into you. You've probably never realized *how much control of your own life* you have handed over to people and circumstances.

> ***People do what they want to do -***
> ***nothing more, nothing less.***

Repetition is the greatest **teacher** or the greatest **torture!** You can gain control of your life if you begin to unplug from the Rejection Connection.

The chart on the next page will help identify the Energy Thieves in your life. Begin by going as far back in time as you can recall and list the people and circumstances that have caused bitterness in you. As you continue reading, you'll be given the *tools to disconnect* from your Energy Thieves once and for all!

EMOTIONAL ENERGY THIEVES

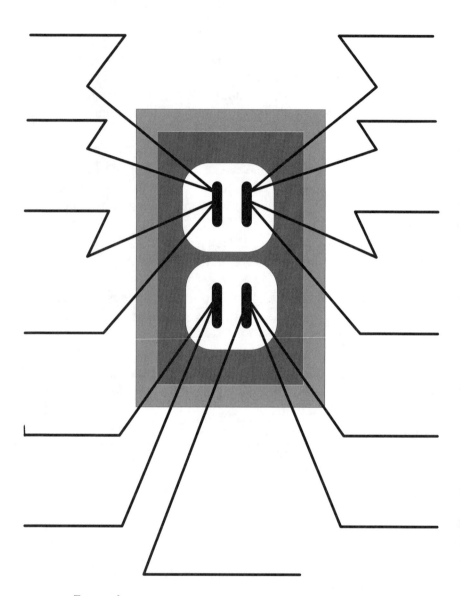

I CAN'T BREAK THE PATTERNS OF THE PAST
UNTIL I'M FREE FROM THE PEOPLE OF THE PAST.

What connects people and circumstances to the past?

List as many of your Emotional Energy Thieves as possible.

MENTAL MORSEL
*"I can't break the patterns of the past until
I'm free of the people of the past."*

12

THE EMOTIONAL PATTERNS OF A PROSTITUTE

The Honeymoon

The casino was crowded and the atmosphere was electrifying. Janet and Richard were on the last leg of a four-day honeymoon to Las Vegas. Richard was tired. Janet was wired. Richard wanted to go to the room for some peace and quiet. Janet hugged her new husband and told him she wanted to walk around to some other casinos to 'soak up the last bit of fun' she could.

It was too early for her to even think about going to their room, especially with Richard. Janet was in a quandary about what to do. She realized she had married a man she didn't love. He was a very nice person, but too quiet and passive for Janet. The only reason she'd married him was to placate her father. To her father, Richard was the epitome of stability and financial security he'd always wanted for his daughter. To Janet, Richard was a bore - pure and simple.

As Janet related her story to me, I learned she'd been raised in a minister's home. Her father was dominant, extremely hostile, and intolerant. Janet had been the target of her father's verbal and emotional abuse during her teen years. She was devastated by his angry tirades of name-calling. Even though they were never close, Janet still always wanted to win her father's approval. Eventually, Janet's rebellion towards her father equaled his anger. To escape, she'd run away from home for days at a time, but soon would quietly recant and return home to protect the family's reputation.

Janet was a petite, vivacious little spitfire of a woman, who turned the heads of many young men. Her self image, though, had been destroyed. Wearing something as simple as jeans and a tube top would incite her dad to call her names such as whore, slut, or streetwalker. Janet was always put down for the makeup she wore, the friends she had, and the places she went.

Janet could not remember her father ever hugging her or telling her he loved her. Starved for affection, Janet became very promiscuous. After graduation from high school, she hit the high road and left home for good, or so she thought. After several months of struggling to make it on her own, she gave up and resigned herself to become the good little girl her father wanted. She moved back home, got a job, and settled down. Within a year she was married to Richard and finally won her father's approval.

Richard was one of the 'good boys' in the church. He taught Sunday School, sang in the choir, never missed services, had a promising career, and was totally dedicated to the Lord. Now her father was pleased and she was married to a man she didn't love.

The sights and sounds of Vegas were exhilarating. Meandering from casino to casino, Janet would stop to visit with people playing the slot machines. Then she noticed him. A slim, good-looking, middle-aged man with a cute grin. As their eyes met, Janet felt a new rush of excitement. He was handsome, outgoing, and intriguing. After brief introductions, they moved toward a quiet lounge where they could have a drink and get better acquainted.

Janet was thrilled with his attentiveness and sensitivity. The fact that he was married and had several children was not important to her. For now, he was hers and she was his. After a few hours, Janet and the stranger went to his room.

The rest of the story is obvious.

It was 1:00 a.m. when Janet tiptoed into her and Richard's hotel room. She felt like a teenager sneaking back into the house after being out past curfew. There was the rush of fear and apprehension. She just knew her husband would be worried sick or angry. When she saw him snoring in front of the TV, her fear left her and she became disgusted. "How boring," she thought as she looked at her sleeping husband.

That night began a series of quickie affairs for Janet. By the sixth month of her marriage, Janet had 'met' four strangers, all of them attentive, strong, aggressive and exciting.

It wasn't long before Janet wanted out of the marriage. She felt trapped - a prisoner of boredom. To make matters worse, Richard refused to go to counseling. "You're the one with the problem," he said. "*You* need to get it fixed."

Janet was a *Rejection Junkie!* How could she fix a problem she didn't understand? Janet's father had sexually abused her on a verbal, non-physical level when he'd call her names like whore and slut. Now the prophecy was being fulfilled. Janet was recycling the rejection from her father and Richard had become the victim of the second order.

Janet had the emotional patterns of a prostitute.

Why would any man or woman become a prostitute, walking the streets and selling their bodies? Why would anyone allow himself or herself to become a sexual garbage receptacle for the human race? Contrary to what most people think, it's not for the money; it's not for the fame, and it's definitely not for the job security!

The underlying reasons anyone becomes a prostitute are revenge, power, acceptance and self-destruction.

119

The unspoken messages behind the actions are:

Revenge
"*I'll get even with you.* I'll do what I want with my body, with anyone, anywhere, and any way I want!"

Power
"*I will control you.* I will do what I want with you!"

Acceptance
"*Let's make a deal.* I'll give you my body and you give me acceptance, admiration, and approval."

Self-Destruction
"*Use me, abuse me.* I'm not worth anything, I have no value."

We don't have to be victims of sexual abuse or actually prostitute our bodies to have the emotional patterns of a prostitute. Every client I've counseled has identified with at least one or more of these emotional patterns.

Janet identified with all four of these patterns. She wanted revenge against her father, power over her body, acceptance from men, and was self-destructing through her affairs.

The sexual abuse victim carries emotional scars that last a lifetime.

Let's Talk About Sexual Abuse
The three most common types of sexual abuse are verbal or non-physical, molestation, and incest.

Verbal or non-physical sexual abuse is typified by Janet's father's comments about her body or sexual behavior. Often girls become the objects of sexual slurs or jokes, especially young girls who are beginning to develop. This type of abuse doesn't have to be verbal and can include inappropriate looks, winks, stares, and other body language intended to focus on a person's body or sexual behavior. One client told me her father never touched her physically, but told her often "I love you, but not like a father should love his daughter." She cringed every time he said it.

Molestation is a physical, sexual experience that can take place with anyone, even family members. It can include fondling the genitals or other private areas of the body, indecent exposure, or any variation of unnatural physical contact, such as a neighbor, teacher or babysitter kissing children fully on the mouth in a sexual manner.

Incest is any of these behaviors, primarily sexual intercourse, between members of the same family.

No matter the level or type of abuse, the results are equally destructive and traumatic.

It's Not An Easy Situation!
To make matters worse, many people, even government and church leaders, turn away from the plight of the victim and quietly accept the situation. Why? What reason would anyone have for not wanting to expose a sexual deviant? Rejection! What if the person you were about to expose was your spouse, a close friend, pastor, priest, politician, policemen, grandfather, father or uncle? If the victimizer's actions are brought out into the open, the entire family may be embarrassed (rejected!).

Why do so many of the victims remain quiet? They often fear not being believed. If they tell, they face the possibility of being rejected by other family members or the community for making such an accusation.

Many mothers face a terrible dilemma. If a father has molested his children, what does the mother do? Expose his crime to the authorities? Suffer public embarrassment or condemnation? There's also the shame she may face at the truth of the downfall of her own marriage. Is this something she wants the pastor and church leaders to know?

The whole family is victimized, suffering in their own private hell of fear, guilt, anger, and moral deprivation. As we've discussed in the Generational Passdown, the emotional impact of incest and molestation is passed onto the victim's children and grandchildren.

When the victim marries, the new mate can become what Janet's husband Richard was, a victim of the second order.

The Children's Story
In an actual case, a young girl was molested by her father. Actual intercourse never took place. Beginning when she was seven, and continuing for six years after that, her father came to her room at night, lay beside her and would lovingly hug her and kiss her cheek. During the embrace, he'd caress her genitals and other areas of her body. As this went on time after time, the girl remained in a silent world of guilt and confusion. "Is this what daddies are supposed to do?" she'd ask herself. "What have I done to make him want to do this to me? Should I tell Mother? Why does my body feel good when he touches me there?"

At age thirteen the girl finally saw a television program about sexual molestation. Now she knew for sure that what had been going on all these years was *not* right. She told her mother who, in response, accused her of knowing better and asked why she didn't stop her daddy from doing it. Why didn't she come to her mother when it started?

Instead of an understanding and compassionate reception of the truth, her mother gave her condemnation and rejection. She was told, "If you didn't want it, you would have stopped it! You are dirty!" The parents began fighting and made the daughter feel it was all her fault. Sadly, sex became ugly and horrible to her. She felt that sex was so bad that she'd never want anything to do with it again.

These negative feelings stayed with her through her young adult life and she remained a virgin until her wedding night. Although her husband was a kind and gentle man, their honeymoon was a tense and frustrating experience for both of them. She hadn't told her new husband of her experiences with her father, afraid if she did tell, he would see her as damaged goods and wouldn't want her. Psychologically, she was in emotional bondage to her father.

Although they somehow made it through the first night, during the next few years of their marriage, sex was a dirty act to her to be endured instead of being a pleasurable and bonding act of love. Gradually her husband wearied of her lack of sexual response. No more Mr. Nice Guy. He became resentful and bitter toward her. After ten years and two children, the relationship had deteriorated to the point where he sought a relationship outside the marriage.

Rejection Recycled
The husband now was recycling the rejection by recreating the relationship his wife had with her father - none! The wife had unconsciously passed the rejection on and her private world of guilt and confusion continued with her husband. Eventually the marriage terminated. Now the two children were deprived of a relationship with their father since he remarried a woman with children of her own.

In counseling with **victims of incest and molestation**, I've observed two basic responses: **extreme sexual promiscuity, or extreme sexual abstinence.**

It seems that very few victims experience normal sexual development. In one case of sexual promiscuity, the victim told me that, as a result of her father's molestation, she felt no personal self worth. Understandably, whenever a boy wanted sex, she'd comply. She feared if she didn't, he would find nothing else of value in her. *Acceptance*: one of the four emotional patterns of a prostitute! By the time she was 22 years old, she'd had sexual relationships with over 40 men! Another pattern: *Self-Destruction.*

Another victim told me because of the incest she'd experienced with her father and brother, she wanted to get even with men. A third pattern: *Revenge.* During her early teens and twenties, she never engaged in sexual intercourse, but would willingly lead men on, just to tease them. The fourth one: *Power.* She rationalized her powerful and revengeful behavior by telling herself, "After all, men are only out for all they can get!" After marriage, she found she could not sexually climax with her husband, so to satisfy herself she masturbated frequently. The revenge factor she had toward men in general, resulted in rejection of her husband and sexual satisfaction with him.

The other extreme response is abstinence. I counseled a victim who was so sexually inhibited she couldn't even stand the thought of a man touching her. She dated only to appear socially normal. When she did eventually develop a fairly stable relationship with a man, she had a nervous breakdown just before the wedding. When the truth became known, her fiancé decided he didn't want to marry her. The young lady in my office told me she never had married after that and planned never to marry in the future. Marriage to her means pain, sex and trauma. In her emotional state, marriage would have been miserable. Sadly, this woman did not respond to therapy and is still living life in emotional and sexual bondage.

Early sexual experiences for both males and females have a long-lasting effect. While the majority of incest victims are female, the trauma for the smaller male percentage is equally devastating. One sixteen-year-old boy had been intoxicated by his mother and coerced into having sex with her. When he came to my office for counseling, all he could do for the first two sessions was weep uncontrollably. In the third session, his anger came out. The guilt, shame, and embarrassment he felt about his experiences were overpowering. He hated women and had been acting out his anger by physically abusing his girlfriend, doing to her what he really wanted to do to his mother but couldn't. His bitterness had become so intense, he would entertain thoughts about killing his mother and then killing himself.

It's not unusual for male victims of incest or molestation to eventually become impotent. Barring relatively rare physical problems, most impotency is psychological as in the following situation.

As a child, one man was forced to watch his brother and sister commit incest. They tried to entice him into joining them, but he refused. There were times, however, when his sister would fondle and tease him and, as a result, he never had a good feeling about sex. As he grew up, he just plain wasn't interested. When he married, the first few years of his sexual relationship with his wife were described as merely 'all right'. Today he is impotent. Sex is just too much of an effort.

Another response to incest and sexual molestation is homosexualism (the sexual activity) or homosexuality (the condition). Homosexuals are *not* born - they are *made*, despite the increasing claims of today's gay community activists. Most homosexuals have emotional problems stemming from an addiction to rejection. Most homosexuals are *Rejection Junkies!*

Many women are drawn to the emotional and sexual comfort of lesbianism because of past sexual and emotional rejection from one or both of their parents. The reverse is also true, with male homosexuals drawn to other men because of rejection from one or both of their parents.

More often than not, the victimizers themselves have been rejected, if not sexually, at least emotionally. Incapable of developing healthy relationships, these people enter a world of abusing others and even themselves. They have no feeling for the agony of their victims because the pounding of their own pain and rejection is too strong.

In counseling child molesters, I've come to the conclusion that the most significant underlying cause for this behavior is the feeling of power and acceptance they get from their victims. Why? Because the molesters are Rejection Junkies in the process of passing their rejection on to their victims.

Freedom For All
If you or someone you know has been a victim of incest, I encourage you to seek counseling. Both the victim and the victimizer need help.

If you are a victim, you no longer have to live with the fear and guilt because of what's happened. There is freedom to be found - *just for you!*

If you are a victimizer, seek help for your own sake. You no longer have to live in a world of rejection and shame. You, too, can *gain your freedom!*

List the four emotional response patterns of a prostitute.

List the three types of sexual abuse.

List the two basic responses to sexual abuse.

Mental Morsel

*"Freedom from the pain of the past
brings peace to the present."*

13

A Soul at War

Imagine for a moment that you begin to have trouble seeing. When you visit the optometrist, he examines you and prescribes corrective lenses as the solution to your problem. After a few months, your vision becomes worse. This time you leave the optometrist's office with a new set of bifocals. For awhile, things look better, but then your vision begins to blur again. A third visit to the doctor sends you home with trifocals.

Something starts to be drastically wrong, though. You get headaches and are seeing black spots. Finally, you consult a specialist. A series of intensive tests reveals that you are suffering from a brain tumor and your optical nerves are slowly being destroyed.

Do you go back to the optometrist for stronger lenses? Of course not! You need surgery to remove the tumor. The tumor is the root of your problem. The failing eyesight is only the symptom.

For counseling to be effective, three things must be accomplished:

We must:
* **IDENTIFY** THE PROBLEM (Not just symptoms)
* **ISOLATE** THE PROBLEM (Not just symptoms)
* **ELIMINATE** THE PROBLEM (Not just symptoms)

When we treat only the symptoms, and not the root problem, we're like the optometrist dispensing Band-Aid therapy that is only temporary. We may be fooled into thinking everything will be okay when, in reality, the problem is only growing worse. You know what happens in the medical field when the real problem is not corrected: the longer the problem exists, the worse it gets, and if not treated may lead to death. The same is true for our mental and emotional health.

Christians in conflict are continually being told to 'pray about it', 'turn it over to the Lord', 'get right with God', and to 'die to self'. This Band-Aid mentality is not effective because it does not approach *the totality of man*.

The Triunity of Man

Let's look at the scriptural truth of the 'triunity of man'. We know that man was created in God's image. "And God said, Let us make man in our image, after our likeness:" Genesis 1:26a. "So God created man in His own image, in the image of God created He him; male and female created He them." Genesis 1:27a.

To be "created in God's image" doesn't mean we left our mother's womb with a long white beard or nail holes in our hands. It means that, like God, we are *triune* or three-in-one.

God is Father, Son and Holy Spirit. Man is body, soul and spirit. This truth can only be accepted and understood by the enlightenment of God's Word, the Bible. "For the word of God is quick, and powerful, and sharper than any two-edged sword, piercing even to the dividing asunder of soul and spirit, and of the joints and marrow (body), and is a discerner of the thoughts and intents of the heart." Hebrews 4:12.

The Word of God will enable you to discern where the root cause of your conflict lies. Is your conflict centered in your body, your soul, or your spirit?

The Spirit of Man

Referring to the graphic on the opposite page, your spirit is comprised of three elements:

> *Intuition:* That mysterious ability you have of quick and ready knowledge.
> *Conscience:* That part of you that says, "This is right, that is wrong."
> *Fellowship:* That part of you that communicates with the Lord.

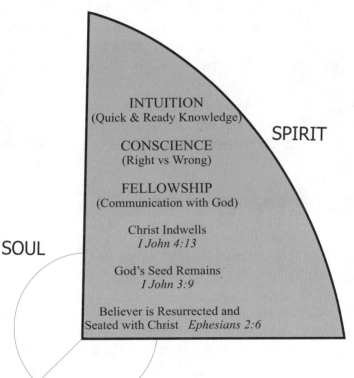

SOUL

SPIRIT

INTUITION
(Quick & Ready Knowledge)

CONSCIENCE
(Right vs Wrong)

FELLOWSHIP
(Communication with God)

Christ Indwells
I John 4:13

God's Seed Remains
I John 3:9

Believer is Resurrected and
Seated with Christ *Ephesians 2:6*

BODY

The person without Christ is dead spiritually. The person with Christ is alive spiritually. "Hereby know we that we dwell in Him, and He in us, because He hath given us of His Spirit. " I John 4: 13. When I accepted Christ as my Savior, He came to dwell in me in His Spirit. His Spirit is perfect. His Spirit is complete. All of his Spirit dwells in me, not just a part. He dwells in me and I dwell in Him.

If His Spirit dwells in me and I dwell in Him, then where is my old, dead spirit? *In Christ,* in heavenly places! "But God, who is rich in mercy, for his great love wherewith He loved us, even when we were dead in sins, hath quickened us together with Christ, *by grace ye are saved*; and hath raised us up together, and *made us sit together in heavenly places in Christ Jesus.*" Ephesians 2:4-6.

Imagine that! My spirit that was 'dead in trespass and sin' has been supernaturally resurrected with Christ in heavenly places. His death became my death. His burial became my burial.

His resurrection became my resurrection!

Where is Christ? In me! Where am I? In Christ, in heavenly places! As Jesus sits at the right hand of the Father, I sit with the Father too.

I'm sure when you awoke today you didn't jump out of bed and shout, "Good morning, Lord! I'm in heavenly places today!" If you're like many people, most mornings you get out of bed and moan, "Good Lord! It's morning!" and wish you could crawl back under the covers.

Every Christian can have a little bit of heaven while still on earth. How? Accept the fact that **you are perfect and spiritually complete**! "Whosoever is born of God doeth not commit sin; for his seed remaineth in him: and he cannot sin, because he is born of God." I John 3:9.

That's a verse I avoided for years. I simply couldn't accept the fact that as a believer I was sinless. The key lies in understanding what 'God's seed' is. The original Greek word for this word *seed* is *sperma* (sper'-mah), indicating something sown.

God's seed is different from man's seed - God's is spiritual, not physical; God's seed brings life, not death, and God's seed is eternal, not temporary.

The person 'born of God' is not capable of sinning *in their Spirit*. The believer's spirit is quickened and resurrected with Christ and God's Spirit dwells in them. They cannot sin *spiritually* because they are born *spiritually* of God. The perfect Spirit of God replaces the imperfect spirit of man. The exchange is complete and we are perfect spiritually.

So where *is* the sin? Where *is* the conflict? Where *is* the problem? In the *soul.*

Where The Problem Is: The Mind, Emotions and Will
Please refer to the graphic on the next page. Your soul is comprised of three basic elements:

Mind:	What you *KNOW* to be true
Emotions:	What you *FEEL* to be true
Will:	The *ABILITY TO RESPOND* to life and its circumstances

Herein lies the problem:

> When what you **KNOW** *(your mind)*
>
> and how you **FEEL** *(your emotions)*
>
> are in conflict,
>
> your **ABILITY TO RESPOND** *(your will)*
>
> will be damaged.

Let's look at some common examples:

I **KNOW** God loves me,

but I don't **FEEL** like He loves me.

I **KNOW** my spouse loves me,

but I don't feel like he/she loves me.

I **KNOW** I can do it,

but I don't **FEEL** like I can do it.

I **KNOW** I'm successful,

but I don't **FEEL** like I'm successful.

I **KNOW** I'm a good parent,

but I don't **FEEL** like a good parent.

And so the conflict between mind and emotions goes.
What we **KNOW** and what we **FEEL** are at war!

Your soul is at war *within* and *against* the Spirit of God that dwells in you.

Like two gears that grind against each other over a long period of time, something will eventually break down.

Instead of responding to life's circumstances with love, joy and peace, the soul-at-war responds with anger, false guilt, depression, anxiety, worry, aggression, withdrawal, sexual conflicts, addictions, feelings of insecurity, inferiority, and inadequacy.

How Christians are Being Misled
Christians are confused. Christians are being misled. They are being told their problems are spiritual in nature and that

if they would only 'die to self' or 'crucify self', things would get better.

Let's examine this false assumption for a moment.

Where in the Bible did God give a direct command to anyone to die to self? No where.

God does say, "Knowing this, that our old man is crucified with Him, that the body of sin might be destroyed, that henceforth we should not serve sin." Romans 6:6.

What happens when you become a Christian? The 'old (nature of) man' is crucified. Crucifixion brings death. How can you die to self when your old self is already dead? Dead people can't die. If the old nature is dead, what's the problem?

Christians Are Creatures of Habit
Have you ever seen frog legs twitching, jumping and flexing in a skillet? Are they dead? Yes! But they still act (respond) as if they are alive.

Ever cut off a snake's head? The body keeps crawling around, thinking it's still alive. Is the snake dead? Of course. But it still acts (responds) as if it is alive.

What about the proverbial chicken with its head cut off? That headless critter races around in circles until suddenly it just drops over. Was the chicken dead before it dropped? Yes! The body was just responding as if it were still alive.

The same is true of our 'old nature' which is already dead.

Let me illustrate. Before I became a Christian I had a problem with anger, depression, and anxiety. After I became a Christian, I still had the exact same problems with anger,

136

depression, and anxiety. Was my old nature dead? Of course. I just kept on *acting* as if it were alive. Even though the old sin nature in my spirit was dead, the mental and emotional **habits** of the old nature continued to control me. I was *spiritually free,* but was still in **mental and emotional bondage** to the habits of the old nature!

My **soul** (mind, emotions and will) was at war with the Spirit of God within me. I knew I was saved, but I didn't *feel* like I'd been saved. I knew God loved me, but sometimes I just didn't *feel* like He did.

Why? I'd never had a healthy relationship with my earthly father because it had been full of rejection. So I was *responding* to the **knowledge** of my Heavenly Father's love for me through the old habit of **feeling** rejection from my earthly father. How could I feel God loved me if I didn't feel Dad loved me? I was filled with bitterness and my *soul* was at war.

At the age of 20, I'd become a Christian but was never taught this truth. Every time I heard the following verse read or preached, I'd embark on a tremendous guilt trip: "Therefore, if any man be in Christ, he is a new creature; old things are passed away, behold all things are become new." II Corinthians 5:17.

I still had problems. All things did not seem new to me. I still lusted after young women, carried hatred toward others, and used the Lord's name in vain. I still had problems with anxiety and depression. Where was this 'newness' others talked about? In my **spirit**!

The problem was in my **soul**, which was warring against the **spirit**. The old habits continued to control my mind and emotions. I simply didn't understand the exchanged life in Christ.

137

So what is the believer to do? "Likewise, reckon ye also yourselves to be dead indeed unto sin, but alive unto God through Jesus Christ, our Lord." Romans 6:11.

Stop trying to commit suicide by crucifixion and accept the fact that your old nature is already dead!

Once I truly "reckoned myself to be dead" and understood what that really meant, my old sin habits began to weaken. When I discovered how to get free from the bondage of bitterness that fed the old habits, they began to disappear!

The reason most Christians have a poor self image is because they believe what others say about them.

They continue to live in bondage to past identities others have placed on them instead of their *identity in Christ.*

Our Identity in Christ
The key question you need to ask yourself is, "Do I accept myself as God accepts me?" He accepts us unconditionally! We should be far more concerned with what God thinks of us than what man thinks.

What *does* God think?

"There is therefore now **no condemnation** to them which are in Christ Jesus." Romans 8:1a. "He hath made us **accepted** in the Beloved." Ephesians 1:6b. "And you that were sometimes alienated and enemies in your mind by wicked works, yet now hath He reconciled. In the body of His flesh through death, to present you **holy** and **unblameable** and **unreproveable** in His sight." Colossians 1:21-22.

God says the believer is without condemnation, accepted in the Beloved, holy, unblameable and unreproveable! That's quite an impressive recommendation.

When you reject yourself, you continue to feed the negative mental and emotional habits of the 'old nature' which is dead.

Rejection of self produces symptoms in the **mind**: fantasies, phobias, abusive thoughts, schizophrenia, and paranoia.

Rejection of self produces symptoms in our **emotions**: anger, fear, depression, false guilt, anxiety, worry, insecurity, doubts, inadequacy, inferiority, aggression, withdrawal, and other conflicts. Sound familiar?

No one can have a proper self image when they look at themselves through man's eyes.

When I refer to a proper self image, I don't refer to a sinful level of conceit and egotism. I'm saying that *Christians should have a grateful understanding and acceptance of who they are and how God made them in His image.*

Man's Body - The Third Entity

The third entity of man's triunity is the physical body. Our body becomes the buffer and reacts to the stress caused by the conflict between mind and emotions: the battlefield, as it were. A soul-at-war will produce many physical ailments some of which are: headaches, migraines, nervous stomach, neck and shoulder spasms, hives, allergies, arthritis, colitis, spastic colon, palpitations of the heart, angina pectoris, shooting pains, dizziness, fainting, sweaty hands and feet, blurry vision, pre-mature graying, loss of hair, wrinkles, backaches, leg aches, that 'tired feeling', sleep disorders, and the list goes on ...

Some of the most recently publicized physical diseases that are a direct result of a soul-at-war are Epstein-Barr syndrome, anorexia nervosa, and bulimia.

The person with Epstein-Barr syndrome might hear his **body** say something like this to his **soul**: "Even though you're on major performance trips to avoid rejection, I can't perform for you any more. I'm just too tired!"

The person with anorexia might hear his **body** say to his **soul**, "You starved me so that you could gain acceptance from man and avoid his rejection. Now my systems are shutting down and soon I will be dead. Please stop!"

The bulimia sufferer's **body** talk goes something like this, "You are so filled with bitterness and hooked on rejection that you have to constantly comfort me with food to **feel** better. Then you force me to get rid of it so you won't be rejected again for being fat. Now I can't keep *anything* down. You're ruining me!"

Do you have physical symptoms that have plagued you over the years?

At New Life Dynamics Christian Counseling Center, our one goal is to enable our clients to eliminate the conflict that occurs between the **mind** (what we *know*) and **emotions** (what we *feel)*.

The two primary tools we depend on are:

The Ministry of God's Word
and
The Ministry of the Holy Spirit

Can a soul-at-war find peace? Can a soul-at-war become Spirit-controlled? *Yes!*

Read on. Chapter Fourteen will help you further understand the concept!

For counseling to be effective, what three things must be accomplished?

What is the 'triunity' of man?

Wherein lies the conflict?

What happens to the old nature at the time of salvation?

Where does the resurrected spirit of man abide?

MENTAL MORSEL

"The reason most Christians have a poor self image is because they believe what others have said about them."

UNDERSTANDING THE CONCEPT

A person whose life is in turmoil can compare the situation to a pot of boiling water. When the water boils, the steam rises. The more intense the heat, the more intense the vapors.

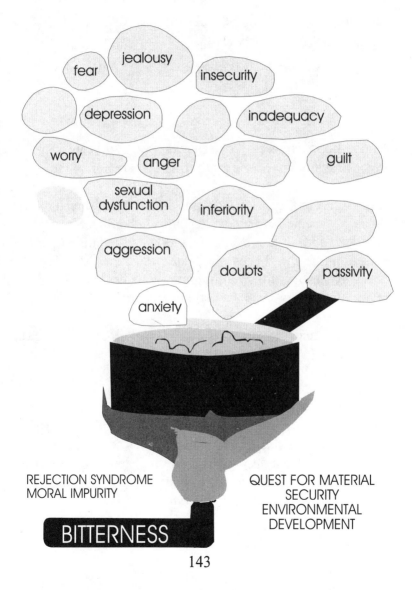

LIFE IN TURMOIL

jealousy · fear · insecurity · depression · inadequacy · worry · anger · guilt · sexual dysfunction · inferiority · aggression · doubts · passivity · anxiety

REJECTION SYNDROME
MORAL IMPURITY

QUEST FOR MATERIAL
SECURITY
ENVIRONMENTAL
DEVELOPMENT

BITTERNESS

Let the vapors represent the symptomatic behaviors in your life. Put a check mark next to each behavior you have experienced or are experiencing.

❑ Fear	❑ Jealousy	❑ Insecurity
❑ Worry	❑ Depression	❑ Inadequacy
❑ Guilt	❑ Sexual Conflict	❑ Anger
❑ Inferiority	❑ Aggression	❑ Doubts
❑ Passivity	❑ Anxiety	❑ Withdrawal
❑ _____	❑ _____	❑ _____

You notice there are several blanks; you may want to fill in specific symptoms you are suffering that are not on the list.

In a counseling session with one lady I asked her how she thought she could get the 'water' to stop boiling. She replied, "Put ice cubes in it!" Well, that works for awhile, but unless we *eliminate* the flames, the water will never stop boiling. How exhausting to go through life endlessly putting ice cubes into the pot, but never solving the problem!

What continues to keep our life in turmoil? The four basic flames are:

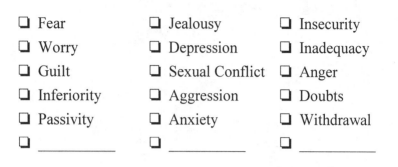 **The Quest for Material Security**

Living and working with a focus only on material desires leads to the sacrifice of many lives at the altar of materialism. Countless marriages and families fall apart when the main focus is to try to make a living with little time or energy spent on building the *quality* of life.

Environmental Development

Our mental and emotional development in early childhood affects us throughout our adult lives. Most adults are in bondage to the circumstances of their childhood.

The Rejection Syndrome

The recycling of rejection in one's relationships keeps a person's life in constant turmoil.

Moral Impurity

Most often associated with sexual misbehavior, moral impurity extends far beyond that limited definition; for example, "a promise made and not kept becomes a lie". Someone else's moral impurity has probably affected you at some time or another.

Are you catching the concept? The water is boiling. The vapors (symptoms) are evident. The four flames are the source of the heat.

Now all we have to do is shut off the *fuel*: **eliminate the bitterness.**

Forget the ice cubes! Without the **fuel** (bitterness), we'd never have any flames. With no flames, no heat. No heat, no boiling (turmoil). No boiling, no vapors (symptoms). It's really quite simple!

What are the four basic flames that create the turmoil in our life?

What is the fuel that feeds the flames?

15

How to Win By Losing

Learning to do the unnatural thing in a natural manner is a principle that Jesus followed.

It's unnatural to love your enemies. It's unnatural to pray for someone who spitefully uses and persecutes you. It's unnatural to bless them that curse you. It's unnatural to do good to those who hate you.

What was natural for Jesus is unnatural for mankind. In fact, it's supernatural.

In the counseling process, much energy is invested in teaching our clients how to do the unnatural thing in a natural manner.

One of the most unnatural things for a person to do is to learn how to *win by losing*.

Christians are barraged with hype to be winners, overcomers, conquerors, and good soldiers for Christ. The concern is legitimate. Consider the following admonishments:

"Nay, in all these things we are more than *conquerors* through Him that loved us." Romans 8:37.

"*Fight* the good fight of faith," I Timothy 6:12a.

"Thou therefore *endure hardness,* as a *good soldier* of Jesus Christ." II Timothy 2:3.

"For whatsoever is born of God *overcometh* the world: and this is the *victory* that *overcometh* the world, even our faith." I John 5:4-5.

"If we *suffer*, we shall also *reign* with Him." II Timothy 1:12a.

"I have *fought a good fight*, I have *finished my course*, I have kept the faith." II Timothy 4:7.

Wow! Reading these particular scriptures sure gets my blood pumping! I want to WIN! I'm a natural-born achiever and when I was born again, I plugged into a supernatural power source. I can say with the apostle Paul that, "I've fought the good fight, run the race, and kept the faith."

My life has included heartaches and heartbreaks. Sometimes it was so bad when I was going downhill that it seemed I would never have a mountaintop experience again.

When it comes to winning, we should be *concerned*, but *not consumed!*

Losing is an important part of life. I never really began to win until I learned the necessity of losing.

Losing to win is unnatural.

Losing to win is not practical.

Losing to win is not sensible.

Losing to win goes against every fiber of common sense I have! Yet, Jesus teaches us that the *only* way to win is to be willing to lose. "For whosoever will save his life shall lose it; but whosoever shall lose his life for my sake and the gospel's, the same shall save it." Mark 8:35.

How to "win by losing" is an oxymoron that grabs your attention. It's not glamorous, popular or sensible, but it reaches your conscience! If you're truly desirous of becoming free from your bitterness, then you'll eagerly embrace this principle:

Bitterness is the rope used in many tug-of-wars.
It keeps the opponents at a safe distance from
each other, yet it keeps them connected.

Letting Go of the Rope

When I was in junior high school, eight of us would play tug-o-war, with four of us at each end of the rope. We needed an extra-long rope because between both sides stretched ol' Charlie Creek, sometimes more of a mudhole than a creek. The losers were always dragged through the cold muddy waters over to the winning side.

This time we were losing. I was the front man on my team, which meant I would get wet first. As soon as I went into the water, the rest of our team would tumble in on top of me. I was getting pretty tired of that and wanted to win somehow. I surveyed the other team. They were good - really good! I knew we'd never win by trying to match their strength. So I called a huddle and I coached our team into letting go of the rope before we got dragged through the water again.

This last tug-o-war really tested our endurance. The rope was burning the palms of my hands and my feet were sliding closer to the water. We pulled with all our might and when it was clear we were going to lose, I hollered, "NOW!" We all let go of the rope.

You should have seen the other team! They all fell backward into each other, hitting the ground hard. Within seconds, they

149

scrambled to their feet and screamed, "Quitters! Cowards!" and a few other choice names. Boy, were they angry!

We were laughing. It was hilarious! It was poetic justice. It was one of those times I'll never forget. We lost - but we WON!

Listen! Pay attention! If you want to win the tug-o-wars of life, sometimes you're going to have to let go of the rope. You need to decide what you're willing to lose, sometimes before the game begins, so you can really win.

Losing to Win is a powerful principle. It's scriptural, sensible, and significant!

Sylvia Lets Go
Early in our marriage, Sylvia and I agreed she shouldn't have the added pressure of paying the bills. We also agreed that neither of us would *assume any responsibility that God did not intend for us to have* in the first place. One day I came home from work and the phone was dead. Apparently it had been disconnected. I asked, "Sylvia, did you know the phone was dead?"

She said, "Yes." I asked, "Sylvia, why didn't you remind me to pay the phone bill?"

She replied, "Remember, we agreed that I would not be your conscience?" Well, I knew that, but I was testing her. I apologized for not paying the phone bill and assured her I would take care of it the next day.

Well, I came home that next evening about 7:00 p.m., picked up the phone, and found it was still dead. This time I hollered at Sylvia!

"Do you realize this phone is still disconnected???" Quietly, she replied, "Yes."

I yelled, "Come on, Sylvia, this is going too far. Why didn't you remind me to pay this bill?"

Quietly, but with conviction, Sylvia said, "I decided that when *you* got tired of not having a phone, you would pay the bill."

Needless to say, I got the message. The bill was paid the next day.

The following week, Sylvia called me at the office and said, "Honey, we have a problem. There's no water in the house."

"Why?" I asked quickly.

"Well, some man was in the front yard and I think he turned it off."

Oh, was I embarrassed! I asked Sylvia to please forgive me, and I assured her I would take care of the matter immediately. I could almost hear the sweet little smile in her voice when she said, "Don't worry about it, Honey. Since I can't cook without water, you'll just have to take us out to dinner."

She wasn't mad. She didn't yell. She didn't cry. She wasn't my conscience. Sylvia had decided she was willing to lose so she could win. She lost the telephone. She lost the water. But she **won** because she allowed *God* to put the pressure on me to be sensitive to her needs. I responded to the pressure and made sure our utilities were never disconnected again.

The Greater Prize

One lady I counseled shared a story of how she *let go of the rope* and allowed the Holy Spirit to put the pressure on her husband. She told me, "Dr. Lawrence, there was something I really wanted, but I let go of it because there was something I wanted *even more*." I asked her to explain and she shared her story.

Rachel and her husband had both been married before. When Rachel married Dan, she became stepmother to his young son. They found they could have no children of their own, so Rachel lavished her love and motherly talents on Dan's son during his frequent visitation with them. When the boy began school, Rachel was looking forward to attending the first parent-teacher conference with her husband and finding out about her stepson's progress.

However, as is frequent in divorce, Dan's ex-wife had remained extremely bitter toward Dan, and particularly at Rachel, whom she blamed for controlling her ex-husband. Dan's ex-wife had been able to get him to go along with all her orders until he'd remarried Rachel. She was also angry that her son was forming a loving bond with his new stepmother. Dan's ex-wife had frequently left angry phone messages, written nasty letters, and had even once threatened to kill Rachel.

When it came time to go to the school and meet with the teacher, Dan knew his ex-wife would also be there. He knew there would be hostility and there could be a scene.

"I really wanted to go to the meeting," Rachel told me. "I'd helped my stepson learn to read and had worked on his homework with him. I wanted to meet the teacher. But Dan was afraid of conflict. He asked me to stay home. He said he'd tell me all about it later."

"That hurt, Dr. Lawrence", she continued. "I could have insisted and gone anyway. I knew I could have talked him into it if I pushed long and hard enough." Instead, Rachel decided to tell her husband how she felt and that she needed him to be sensitive to her needs and overcome his fear of conflict. Then she decided to *let go* of the rope and let the Holy Spirit put pressure on her husband's conscience. She stayed home.

Dan went alone to the meeting where his ex-wife's behavior ranged from caustic and controlling, to almost giddy because she had her ex-husband beside her again without his new wife. As he sat in the conference, he began to regret asking his wife to stay home. He'd realized Rachel had been a big part of his son's life and should have been included. He also began to realize that he no longer belonged at the side of his bitter ex-wife.

"I wanted something *more* than just being able to go to the meeting," Rachel advised me. "I wanted my husband to begin to learn where his priorities were and to face his fears of conflict. I knew he hadn't really completed the emotional separation from his ex-wife and was still responding to her in old fear-based patterns. I thought if he went without me, it might teach him something."

"I was right," she continued, "Dan came home and told me that I belonged at his side and he would never leave me at home again. He told the teacher that next time he'd like a separate appointment from his ex-wife and the teacher agreed that would be a good idea. That night was the beginning of his real emotional separation from his ex-wife."

Rachel had lost. She didn't get to go to the first parent-teacher conference. She was left out. Rachel had been willing to miss being involved and agreed to accept her husband's authority.

Rachel had lost, yet she had won. She won a husband with an increased sensitivity to her needs and a better understanding of their situation. After that night, Dan began to look at all kinds of new and different options that were available to him in situations involving his ex-wife. Rachel had been willing to lose so she could to win.

The Tale of Two Harlots

Two women stood before a King. Both claimed to be the mother of the baby being held by the soldier. Both were harlots. Both lived in the same house and, within days of each other, had given birth to infant sons.

As one mother slept with her child in her arms, she accidentally laid on him, smothering him to death. Seeing her dead infant, she rose while the other woman still slept, took the living baby from the sleeping mother, and replaced him with her dead child.

Upon waking, the mother of the living child realized immediately the dead child was not hers. Seeking justice, she took the matter before their wise leader, King Solomon.

Each claimed to be the mother, yet neither could prove to whom the baby belonged.

To resolve the conflict, the king ordered the baby to be cut in two with one half going to each of the women. With a broken heart, the real mother appealed to the king and said. "Let the baby live! Let the other woman have him. I'm willing to lose him so he can live."

The mother of the dead infant said, "No! The king's judgment is fair. Let the baby be divided between us!"

The wise king knew immediately who the real mother was. He ordered the soldier to place the baby into his mother's arms.

Are you beginning to understand? Enacting the principle of **losing to win** takes courage, faith, patience, and a meek and quiet spirit.

Holding onto the rope can end up being very painful. You get dragged to where others want you to go. They are in control. You lose control over your own life. Everything and everyone else owns you.

Bitterness is the rope that losers hold on to.
Bitterness is the rope many people hang themselves with.

We'll teach you *how* to let go of the rope in the following chapters.

What attitude consumes many Christians?

Who taught the principle how to win by losing?

Mental Morsel
"We need to learn to do the unnatural
in a natural manner."

16

GRIEVE NO MORE

Everyone grieves.

At some point in our lives, we are *all* in the grieving process. No one is exempt, not even Jesus. He *grieved* as he entered triumphantly into Jerusalem. "And when he was come near, he beheld the city, and *wept* over it." Luke 19:41.

Jesus *grieved* as he stood beside the tomb of his dear friend, Lazarus. "Jesus *wept*." John 11:35. Jesus *grieved* in the Garden of Gethsemane as he prepared for His imminent death. "Then saith He unto them, My soul is *exceedingly sorrowful*, even unto death." Matthew 26:38. Jesus was "despised and *rejected* of men, a man of *sorrows*, and *acquainted with grief*." Isaiah 53:3.

Every person reading this book has this in common with Jesus: you, too, are acquainted with grief.

Grieving is natural, not sinful. "For we have not an high priest which cannot be touched with the feelings of our infirmities; but was in all points tempted like as we are, yet *without sin.*" Hebrews 4:15.

You may be grieving over something even as you read this book. Take heart, though, because ...

Grieving is *normal*!

Grieving is *necessary*!

Grieving is painful, yet *purifying*!

157

Grieving is sad, yet *soul-cleansing!*

Grieving is heart-breaking, yet *healthy!*

Are you grieving over a broken dream? A broken promise? A broken friendship?

Maybe your grief is about a damaged relationship, a divorce, a loss, or detachment of a loved one. Financial pressures or health problems?

No matter the circumstances, grieving , like breathing, is part of life. It's a process. It has a beginning and should have an end. Despite what we've heard all our lives, time alone does *not* heal all wounds.

Many people in their 60's, 70's or 80's are still grieving over things that happened in their childhood. This kind of grieving is not normal, natural, or necessary.

Being 'stuck' in the grieving process, especially when it lasts a lifetime, is nothing more than bitterness which has taken a strong hold and is rooted in the soul of the sufferer.

The Stages of Grief

Bitterness can last a lifetime, but healthy grieving should only last for a limited period of time. Healthy grieving will find the sufferer experiencing several levels of emotional responses as he moves through the grief process. Let's examine the stages of grief.

SHOCK

The beginning of grief says "This can't be happening, I refuse to believe this has happened!" Depending on the severity of the situation, this period can last briefly or for a longer time. Shock should not last a lifetime. If it does, the sufferer eventually refuses to accept reality.

DENIAL

From shock, the person most frequently moves into a period of denial. "I won't! I can't believe this has really happened to me. I refuse to accept it."

This stage is often accompanied by clever rationalizing away the facts. When a person stays in denial for months upon end, he is actually allowing bitterness to take root. Although denial is initially a natural and normal response, it is not necessary and is actually damaging to allow denial to stay. The dangers of navigating the River Denial are staying too long and getting sucked under by the strong undercurrents of bitterness.

ANGER, GUILT, AND GRIEF

Like emotional whirlpools, these are the levels of grieving into which most people move and find themselves being tossed helplessly back and forth.

Anger says: "It's not fair, I don't deserve this!"
Guilt says: "What could I have done? What should I have done?"
Grief says: "I'm hurting. Part of me is dying."

As life continues, and other tragedies add more grief, the cycle intensifies: more anger, more guilt, more grief. More *bitterness*! When we allow the bitterness to pull us under, it drowns any hope, joy or peace we might have.

Where are you now in your life? Troubled? Defiled? Any resemblance of the innocent child you used to be has been distorted by bitterness. It's time to move on.

ACCEPTANCE

Acceptance says, "It happened and it happened to me." This change of attitude is only possible once bitterness has been done away with. Acceptance leads to release.

RELEASE

Release says, "I can accept that this happened and I know that it no longer needs to control me. That part of my life is in the past. I choose to let go and focus my energies on other areas of my life." Release leads to recovery.

RECOVERY

This final stage of the grieving process says, "I will establish new goals and desires for my life." It is here that we are able to say with the Apostle Paul, "This one thing I do, forgetting those things which are behind, and reaching forth unto those things which are before." Phillippians 3:13b.

ACCEPTANCE leads to

RELEASE leads to

RECOVERY

What is the hinge that recovery swivels on? **Getting free from your bitterness.**

List the levels of grieving.

What are the three most frequently cycled levels of grieving?

What is the key to bringing grieving to an end?

MENTAL MORSEL
"Grieving, like breathing, is part of life.
It has a beginning and it should have an end."

17

THE EMOTIONAL SURGERY

In the previous chapters of this book, you've learned seven basic truths:

Truth One
Most emotional bondage is developed
during the first eight years of a person's life.

Truth Two
Emotional bondage is given birth by the root of bitterness.

Truth Three
Bitterness is passed down from one generation to the next to
the third and fourth generations.

Truth Four
Rejection recycles itself in relationships with others.

Truth Five
Everyone experiences rejection in some form.
Some experience and assimilate rejection so much,
they become *Rejection Junkies.*

Truth Six
The Rejection Syndrome is the underlying cause of mental
and emotional turmoil, barring any physiological problems.

Truth Seven
A person cannot break the patterns of the past until he is free
from the people of the past.

This chapter will bring you another truth, the most important of all:

How to gain your mental and emotional freedom and break the rejection habit!

Following are the five basic steps that will help you eliminate the mental and emotional turmoil that has controlled your life. This process is called 'Emotional Surgery' because, unlike Band-Aid therapy, the root of bitterness can be completely cut from your life like a tumor is cut away.

Are you ready? Are you sincere? Do you really want your freedom?

If the answer is YES!, then follow these steps:

STEP 1: REVIEW YOUR LIFE HISTORY
Action
Make a list of every single person, thing, or circumstance which has wounded your spirit, or that you have become bitter toward for any reason.

Understand this: Bitterness comes in many forms. It is most often thought of as an outward anger or hatred, but more often it's a deep, inward resentment or hurt. Go back to Chapter 3 to review all the forms which bitterness may take.

Bitterness is not limited to people. Other things to which we've responded in bitterness can include inanimate objects such as houses, cars, clothes, money, ideals, fantasies, circumstances, addictions, jobs, animals, religious beliefs, denominations, institutions, even parts of our own body which have failed us in some way.

As you compile your list of names, be sure to include deceased persons and those whom you may never see again, not just those you deal with on a day-to-day basis. Particularly include people you avoid. This list must be complete. The purpose of the Emotional Surgery is to *identify, isolate, and eliminate* every tentacle of the root of bitterness.

Remember: **You cannot break the patterns of the past until you're free from the people of the past.**

The next four steps are called Action Therapy. You will be taking action to provide the therapy your soul needs.

STEP 2: 'PUT YOUR POTATOES
IN THE BACK OF THE WAGON'
Action

You will be talking to as many people as possible on the list you have just completed. Before you talk to each person on your list, pray this prayer:

"Lord, please help me turn the responsibility of (person's name) response over to you, so I don't come away feeling guilty or rejected."

Let God take care of their response. You focus on your own attitude. If you don't turn their response over to the Lord, you will come away feeling guilty, rejected, angry, and hurt. Conflict will arise and the next step of your action therapy will be null and void.

The following story illustrates the principle of 'putting your potatoes in the back of the wagon'.

A poor farmer struggled under a large sack of potatoes he carried on his shoulder. Since the market was several miles from his small farm,

165

and he had no beasts of burden or wagon, he started to walk the long road, as usual, by himself. Along the way, he stopped to rest and soon a neighbor approached him in a wagon. The driver stopped and asked the poor farmer if he'd like a ride. Gratefully, the man accepted. After climbing up into the wagon seat, he bent down, and with a great strain, lifted the sack of potatoes up onto his shoulder. Surprised, the driver said, "You can put your potatoes in the back of my wagon." The poor farmer responded, "Oh thank you, but you've already been so kind to give me a ride, I can't expect you to carry my potatoes, too."

Sound familiar?

Why is it we continue to carry our bitterness like a heavy burden? Old habits! Some Christians have been dutifully carrying their 'sack of potatoes' so long that it's filled with a rotten and contentious odor! Every once in awhile, they turn their head to get a whiff of the nasty smell to assure themselves they are still 'suffering for Jesus'. That is neither freedom nor abundant life!

It's time for you to put your potatoes in the back of the wagon. The most important and painful part of the Emotional Surgery is when you ask each person on your list to forgive *you* for your bitterness toward him or her.

You may say, 'The past is in the past, why bring all that stuff up again now?" Well, guess what? You're NOT going to bring up anything from the past when you complete this part of the action therapy. *You're simply going to ask forgiveness for your own bitterness.* You see, it's time to let go of what they've done to you. It's not what they've done to you that's the problem. **It's your response to what they've done that's the problem: your bitterness!**

Don't be afraid. Don't worry about their response. Put your potatoes in the back of the wagon *by turning their response over to the Lord!*

STEP 3: SEEK FORGIVENESS FOR YOUR BITTERNESS
Action

Here's what to say when you seek forgiveness for your bitterness:

"(Person's Name), the reason I'm talking to you is I've been having some emotional problems. The Lord has revealed to me that part of my problem is that I need to ask you to forgive me for something. (Pause) Would you forgive me for my bitterness toward you?"

Forgive and forget. How many times have you heard *that* old lie? It's impossible to forget if you have bitterness. It's impossible to really forgive if you're still bitter. You will never find the words 'forgive' and 'forget' anywhere in the same verse in the Bible.

Here's another famous lie: "Be like Jesus and forgive." Impossible if we're bitter! Jesus was perfect. In spite of all that mankind did to Him, Jesus chose never to become bitter. Sweet water and bitter water cannot flow through the same fountain. If you are still bitter, you are not free to forgive.

FORGIVENESS: "Becoming more concerned for the needs of the offender than what he has done to offend you."

When you are bitter toward a person, you are certainly not concerned for his needs. Your bitterness has put you in bondage to that person. Here's an example:

A pastor's wife approached me while I was giving a seminar and advised, "That lady over there is angry with you." When I asked why, I found out the lady felt I had been purposely avoiding her. When I had a minute, I approached the lady, introduced myself and said, "I understand you are angry with me." She replied, "You bet I am!" I asked her to share the reason she was upset. "You may not remember me", she said, "But I remember you! Two years ago you were here and ..." she then continued to unload two years' worth of pent-up bitterness that she'd felt toward me. I learned that my offense was that I had interrupted a conversation she'd been having. I continued to listen quietly.

When she stopped talking I asked her to forgive me for offending her in that manner. She stared at me for a moment, started to cry, then said, "I don't think I can forgive you, because if I forgive you, then I'll have to ask you to forgive me!"

I realized at once this woman had carried a huge load of bitterness and for two years had been in mental and emotional bondage to me. I asked, "How much longer do you want to go on being my emotional slave?" Surprised, she asked, "What do you mean?" I asked her who she thought of every time she saw a pastor on TV, or heard on the radio. Her reply was, "You, of course!" I then explained to her that because of her bitterness toward me, I had controlled her mentally and emotionally for the past two years. I further explained that as long as she was bitter, she would not be free to forgive me until she sought forgiveness for her own bitterness. I was her master and she was my slave!

Sweet water and bitter water cannot flow through the same fountain. This poor lady had worked herself up into a nervous condition because of something I had unknowingly done two years in the past. With tears she asked me to forgive her for her bitterness. I forgave her and again asked for forgiveness for my own offense. She forgave me and we hugged.

> ## YOU CANNOT FORGIVE
> ## UNTIL YOU SEEK FORGIVENESS
> ## FOR YOUR OWN BITTERNESS.

Wow! What a powerful truth!

You see, it's not what others have done to you that matters. IT'S YOUR RESPONSE TO THEIR ACTIONS that is important. Although bitterness is a normal human response, you must decide how long you will let it control you.

STEP 4: FOCUS ON *YOUR* ATTITUDE, NOT *THEIR* ACTIONS
Action
No matter what their response may be, the *only* response you are to make is:

"It's not what you have done, it's that I've had the wrong attitude." (Repeat this a second time if necessary.)

Sometimes their response may be, "What have I done to make you bitter?" "What are you talking about?" "When did I ever do anything wrong to you?" "I've tried to be a good mother.." (father, friend, partner).

169

You might hear something like "I did my best! I can't understand why you would be bitter toward me!" No matter what they say, **do not discuss** what they have done to make you bitter. More likely than not, they'd get defensive and draw you into an argument.

You're not there to be their conscience. You're not there to discuss the past, the details, or anything else. You are there to take responsibility for your own attitude and to seek their forgiveness. Period. It's helpful to repeat your first response, keeping the discussion from getting off track:

"It's not what you've done; it's that I've had the wrong attitude."

They're magic words. Powerful. Honest. Simple. Freeing. By repeating these words, you are **assuming responsibility for your own attitude**, and no longer focusing on their action.

Your desire is to get free from the bitterness in your soul, not to rehash the past.

Remember: *"When I focus on my attitude, I cease to focus on others' actions."*

STEP 5: LAYING THE FALSE GUILT AND REJECTION AT THE OTHER PERSON'S FEET
Action

If they have not forgiven you, keep asking a second and third time. If after the third time, they still have not forgiven you, say this calmly but firmly:

"Before I called you, I turned your response over to the Lord. I will not leave this conversation feeling guilty or rejected by you."

170

You may have to quietly hang up if they continue to try to draw you into an argument.

Tell them you have to go now and say goodbye. Don't stay on the phone trying to get them to say what you want. The longer you stay on the phone, the greater the likelihood that you may end up in an argument or some other non-productive discussion.

You Are Not Responsible for Their Response
One client I counseled had to seek forgiveness from her suicidal mother. She became distraught because she feared the action therapy might upset her mother to the point of actually committing suicide. Denise had a good reason to be concerned because her older brother had actually killed himself in his late teens. Denise's mother had also always told her children, "You kids are going to be the death of me! I might as well commit suicide."

Denise's choice was difficult: to get emotionally free or continue to be controlled by her fears.

Denise hated her mother but visited every day to check on her. Why? Denise knew she'd *feel* responsible if her mother did commit suicide. Denise was assuming responsibility for her mother's mental and emotional wellbeing.

After putting off the action therapy for two weeks, Denise finally made the call and, as expected, her mother did flip out. After patiently asking for forgiveness the third time, Denise said, *"Mom, before I called I turned over your response to the Lord, and I will not leave this conversation feeling guilty or rejected by you any longer!"*

Bravo! Denise took the guilt, fear and rejection of a lifetime back to the source: her mother. Denise truly did 'put her potatoes in the back of the wagon'.

171

It's important that you do the same. Remember: Before you speak to each person on your list, pray the prayer out loud, and mean it sincerely from your heart.

Oh, by the way, Denise's mother did not commit suicide.
Now that you understand the five basic steps, the following suggestions will help you in making the action therapy as effective as possible.

* Do as much of your action therapy as possible over the phone. You need to have privacy and safety as you have your script in front of you. You'll probably be nervous and tense. That's okay!

* If you're married, **do not** talk to anyone on your list until you've sought forgiveness from your spouse. **Do not** talk to anyone on your list without your mate beside you. If you are married and desire to reconcile differences, you'll not only experience a freedom from the person you've been bitter toward, but you and your mate will experience a new emotional attachment as you do action therapy together. This is called *emotional transference*.

* Have a meek and quiet spirit. Meekness is not weakness; it is strength under control.

* If a person on your list is a child, try to sit in a position lower than the child is while you're talking. This will capture his or her attention and help keep the child from feeling intimidated.

* Remember: The person from whom you are seeking forgiveness has been a victim of the Rejection Syndrome and will not understand what you are doing. Because he or she is addicted to rejection, the person may reject you

again. So be ready but don't react to it. *Do not try to counsel him or her!*

* Do not determine the success or failure of your action therapy by your *feelings*. Everyone is different. You may experience extreme emotions ranging from anger or depression, to delight, joy, and peace. Go with **what you know**, not **how you feel**. Your emotions will change. Ground yourself in truth.

Dealing With People You May Never See Again
It may have been years since that person you have been bitter toward has died. I have counseled many people who were still in bondage to someone in the grave. Remember emotional energy thieves? Emotional cords from cadavers can still drain the living. People 'plugged in' to the dead by bitterness often ask themselves, "Could I have done something different?" or, "If only the deceased person would have done or said something different, it would all be okay." It's time to leave the dead with the dead and get on with LIFE!

Select a time and place to be alone. Sit down and write a letter as if you were talking to the deceased. Get those buried feelings out. Tell them how they hurt you and how you felt. Express your fear, anger, guilt, or hatred. Use words that really express yourself. Knock off your piety and 'let it rip'! Assume that the deceased could read your letter. Now, I don't believe in communicating with the dead, but I do believe in your expressing all those feelings that death has robbed you of being able to express. It may take thirty minutes or it may take five hours. Depend on the Holy Spirit to minister to you as He cleanses your soul.

I promise you that if you're sincere, you will experience deep emotions and a freedom you never believed possible!

After you get everything out in the letter, ask that person to forgive you for your bitterness toward them. Put your letter in an envelope and mail it! By that I mean, give the letter to a spouse or an intimate friend. Ask them to read it and then to do whatever they want with it - burn it, tear it up, but most importantly, **never let you read it again**. If possible, I encourage you to take the letters to the gravesite. If the contents are such that you don't want anyone else to read it, tear it up in little pieces, find a private place, and throw it to the wind, verbalizing, *"Lord, thank you for setting me free from my bitterness!"*

Use this same basic approach for people who may be alive but whom you will never see again, or are unable to contact. But don't use the excuse that they moved to the other side of town and you don't have their phone number. Get it! Call information. Do a little detective work. If you **really** want to be free, you'll work at getting in touch with as many of the people on your list as possible. Action therapy is most effective when you hear the live voice on the other end of the line.

It works! I have seen many souls in bondage to the deceased and to those in the long, long past gain their freedom with the action therapy.

The Emotional Surgery will *set you free* from the Rejection Syndrome, but you must also *begin **immediately*** to break the negative patterns, responses, and habits which have controlled you.

The next chapter brings even more help!

List the four steps to Action Therapy in the 'Emotional Surgery'.

List five of the seven truths you've learned reading this book.

What prohibits you from forgiving others?

Give the definition of forgiveness.

MENTAL MORSEL
"The problem is not my problem.
My response to the problem becomes my problem."

18

NEVER AGAIN!

Consider the old saying for a moment: "First time, shame on you. Second time, shame on me!"

Since I have gained my freedom from others by following the principles outlined in this book, and have been experiencing life without all the emotional baggage from my past, I am committed to *never again becoming enslaved* to another human being!

What a shame, though, that so many other people will continue in bondage to others. Some will live a life filled with symptoms of the Rejection Syndrome and their lives will be void of the fruit of the Holy Spirit - no love, no joy, no peace.

Why? These people don't know, or won't admit, they're Rejection Junkies. What a sad existence. The miserable leading the miserable. Their days are filled with conflict and turmoil. They will never enjoy the laughter of life or the fulfillment of freedom.

Why? Because they remain bitter and bitterness defiles. Bitterness makes a person blind with revenge. It steals the character of the champion. It plummets the hero from the pedestal of recognition to the level of resignation. It ruins the optimism of the runner.

Bitterness strangles, smothers, spoils, separates, and smashes relationships. It deteriorates, diminishes, and destroys the successes of life. Bitterness is a monster that lashes out at love. The flame of faithfulness becomes extinguished; lovers lose their loyalty; marriages are mangled; families are flung into chaos; careers crumble, and churches are crushed. The toll that bitterness takes on the lives of its victims is immeasurable.

You, the reader, must ask yourself this question:
"Am I going to keep paying the ransom that bitterness demands or am I willing to do what is recommended in this book?"

If you have thoroughly and sincerely followed the instructions in Chapter 17, then you are ready for this chapter. If not, I don't believe you'll be able to accept the three basic truths contained in this final chapter - truth that only those who are free from bitterness can believe and experience. These truths will help you break the rejection habit and keep you from ever being victimized again.

You may respond, "I have failed so miserably, I'll never be free." Not true! The following paradox contains HOPE for all:

"FAILING IS THE SECRET TO SUCCESS."

Remember Steve in Chapter Nine? He learned that failing does not mean you are a failure.

Look at how many times Abraham Lincoln failed. He ran for and lost many political offices before he was elected President. He failed and failed and failed again, and failed some more and failed and failed and failed some more. One day he woke up and found himself President of the United States of America!

Thomas Edison also failed thousands of times. He personally conducted over 1,400 experiments on the incandescent light bulb. Finally, all his failings led to success that marked his name in history.

The reason this book has been written is because I have failed! I failed as a father. I failed as a husband. I failed financially. I failed many, many ways, but every time I failed I took another step toward success.

Mark this statement deeply into the walls of your conscience:

"No man is a failure because he has failed.
A person becomes a failure only when he lets failing
become the last chapter of the book he is writing."

Have you written the last chapter of the book you're writing? No! Then you're not a failure; you are just on your way to becoming a success! So get on with life and let the pain of the past be parted from you forever.

Protecting Your Freedom
When our country declared her independence and gained her freedom, she made sure her borders were protected from ever being captured again. Her armed forces keep constant vigil so that she will never again be taken into bondage. If you have gained your mental and emotional freedom, you'll need also to learn to protect it. The world will always be full of Rejection Junkies and Emotional Energy Thieves who will try to lure you back into bondage by rejecting you. These three truths will help you keep your freedom intact:

TRUTH 1: LEARN TO LOVE YOURSELF
IN THE SAME MANNER GOD LOVES YOU

Impossible? Improbable? Not at all. In fact, God gives these instructions in the Bible: "And thou shalt love the Lord Thy God with all thy heart, and all thy soul, and with all thy mind, and with all thy strength: this is the first commandment. And the second is like, namely this, Thou shalt love thy neighbor as thyself. There is none other commandment greater than these." Mark 12:30-31.

Theologians have argued over this for centuries. Many say that for a person to 'love himself' is carnal and sinful. I totally disagree! Jesus **himself** gave us the commandment, and I think He's more worthy of our trust and respect than any theologian's interpretation.

I'm sure you know, I'm not talking about a conceited, egotistical, prideful type of self-love. I'm talking about a *grateful, loving acceptance of yourself* - the way God accepts you - *just the way you are!*

You may say, "But you don't know the sins I've committed!" You're right, I don't. But God does, and if you've accepted Jesus Christ as your Savior, He has forgiven ALL your sins and cleansed you from ALL unrighteousness.

You cannot accept the creature while you are rejecting the Creator. If you have never become a Christian, I encourage you to pray this prayer:

> *"Lord Jesus, please forgive me of my sins.*
> *Come into my heart and save me.*
> *I receive you as my Savior and Lord.*
> *Please help me to accept myself as you do -*
> *unconditionally!"*

It's time to get off the throne and quit playing God. It's time to see what He sees in you, as He sees it: your purity in Jesus Christ. Because of Him, you have access to complete freedom. The door is open. Step through it and breathe the fresh air of His unconditional love.

Quit beating yourself up for your sin. Enjoy the acceptance He offers. Completely, totally, GOD LOVES US! Wow! What a thrill it is to be FREE from others, FREE from self, ACCEPTED by God, and ACCEPTED by me!

Love, joy, peace.

The inward fruits are

Not just a covering,

but they *remove* the scar.

I'm FREE! Thank God, I'm FREE!

The sun is brighter. The air is fresher. The bird's song is sweeter. My walk is brisker. My step is higher. My love is deeper. Life is livelier and lovelier!

I'm FREE! Thank God, I'm FREE!

A Loving Reflection - Not Rejection

The following technique may sound a little corny at first, but it really works! Get alone in a room with a mirror. Put your face so close to the mirror you can hardly see your face and look deeply into the pupils of your eyes. Look long and deep and don't pull away.

Search for the person you really are. The child. The teenager. The young adult. Get in touch with your soul. Not the face that covers you, or the person you may have become. The real YOU. And when you think you see YOU, tell yourself the following two statements, lovingly and with conviction:

181

I FORGIVE YOU!

No longer are you going to condemn yourself or resent the failings of the past. God has forgiven you and He wants you to accept His forgiveness by forgiving yourself.

I LOVE YOU!

Wow! That's exciting! You are finally accepting and loving yourself and giving yourself the love you may not have felt worthy to receive. *If you can't love and accept yourself, you're not going to be able to love and accept others the way God wants you to.*

TRUTH 2: YOU CAN INSULATE YOURSELF FROM REJECTION WITHOUT ISOLATING FROM IT

Pretty soon, maybe within moments, someone is going to reject you in some way. It's part of life. How will you handle it? You could become a hermit and avoid the human race. You'd certainly be free from rejection, but it's not much fun living alone. Here's what I suggest you do:

Remind yourself constantly that the world is full of Rejection Junkies. Most members of your family and many friends or co-workers are Rejection Junkies. They have the problem - NOT YOU! Remember: It's not what they do or say that matters; it's how you respond that matters!

Receive their rejection, but don't react to it. Our response can be calm now that we're free. No longer do we have to react to the rejection. Shrug it off. If you don't want them to get your goat, don't let them know where it's tied up!

Pray for the Fruit of the Spirit, specifically meekness.
In situations where you know that rejection is likely to
be experienced, prepare yourself by asking for God's
help. Remember, *meekness is not weakness; it's strength
under control!*

Read This Book Ten Times. Get familiar with the
habits of Rejection Junkies so you'll be able to more
quickly identify them. This will help you maintain a
sweet spirit. Give this book as a gift to your family and
friends, then let go. Let the Holy Spirit take over from
there. He's a lot more powerful than we'll ever be!
Don't let others drain you of your emotional energy by
trying to counsel every Rejection Junkie that comes
along. Don't develop a Messiah Complex.

TRUTH 3: LEARN HOW TO HAVE A GRATEFUL SPIRIT

Start learning to appreciate your situation in life. There is a
purpose for every problem that comes along and there is a
healing for every hurt. Believe this and life will take on a
new meaning! In time of trouble, Romans 8:28 is often
referred to by Christians:

> "For we know that *all things* work together for good,
> to those who love God and
> are called according to His purpose."

Not some things, *all things*! What 'good' and what 'purpose'
are being referred to here? The next verse tells us:

"...to be conformed to the image of His Son." Romans 8:29b.
Does that mean we have to be perfect like Jesus is? No!
Does it mean total service, total sacrifice? No!

183

To allow the Holy Spirit's fruits to be *manifested* in our lives is what it means to *be conformed to the character* of Jesus Christ.

"But the fruit of the Spirit is love, joy, peace, long-suffering, gentleness, goodness, faith, meekness, temperance: against such there is no law." Galatians 5:22-23.

Did anyone ever advise you to "live for the Lord"? Well, consider this:

Pious Christians live for the Lord;

Spirit-controlled Christians

let the Lord live through them.

To help you appreciate your situation in life with a joyful heart, begin to pray these three prayers immediately, every day. Write them on a card and carry them with you. Keep them in the bathroom or bring them to work:

1) "Thank you, Lord, for ALL my problems."

Name a few specific problems you're struggling with. Don't just be thankful for the outcome, but for the opportunity to work through them and learn His truths. Many Christians believe problems indicate the presence of sin. Not true! Problems are frames God uses to draw attention to the areas of our lives in which we need help. When you look at all your problems, you'll begin to get an idea of how much time God has invested in framing your life in order to produce a beautiful, finished masterpiece!

Become partners with God in your problems. Until you do, you won't be able to solve them. The Apostle Paul understood this well: "Therefore I take pleasure in infirmities, in reproaches, in necessities, in persecutions, in distresses for Christ's sake: for when I am weak, then am I strong." II Corinthians 12:10. God will allow problems to occur in your life so you can build character qualities that you might lack. Your problems can become your friends!

2) "Lord, I promise to cooperate with you in the lives of others."

When you begin to cooperate with the Lord in the lives of others, it means two things:

Don't allow others to continue to walk all over you while you passively take their abuse. *You may have to isolate yourself from some people to stop the abuse.* Sometimes you must be willing to **lose in order to win.**

Don't be so quick to rescue people from their problems. Get out of the way and let God work his plan in their lives according to His will. Don't become others' conscience.

3) "Lord Help Me to love and accept myself the way You do."

If you have forgiven yourself and love yourself the way God loves you, you'll be able to accept yourself, and others, the way He does.

This book was written to help you *identify, isolate, and eliminate* the cause of the inner turmoil in your life.

My desire is to help you change your life. I hope I have succeeded!

List the three truths that will enable you to maintain your mental and emotional freedom.

Why does God allow problems in our life?

List the three prayers of a positive self image.

Mental Morsel
"I must stop living for the Lord because pious Christians live for the Lord. Spirit-controlled Christians let the Lord live through them."

Dear Reader,

It's been said that things won't change, if things won't change. Your life will stay the same except for two things: the people you meet and the books you read.

Through Rejection Junkies, you have met me and have become acquainted with some of the principles I embrace. These principles have changed my life.

I would like the chance to get to know you too. Perhaps you have a story you would like to share with regards to the impact "Rejection Junkies" has made on your life.

Please contact me by letter at 100 West Clarendon, Suite 1900, Phoenix, Arizona 85013 or by e-mail at info@nld.org. When you contact me, this will enable me to add you to my mailing list.

Thank you for allowing me into your life and, yes, there are other books to follow this one.

God Bless.

Your Friend,

Gary

187